SELL
LIKE THE
BEST

Making Your Goal
Is Easier Than It Looks!

STEPHAN SCHIFFMAN

AMERICA'S #1 CORPORATE SALES TRAINER

BUSINESS

Avon, Massachusetts

D1115448

Published by
Adams Business, an imprint of Adams Media, a division of F+W Media, Inc.
57 Littlefield Street, Avon, MA 02322. U.S.A.
www.adamsmedia.com

ISBN 10: 1-59869-147-3
ISBN 13: 978-1-59869-147-4

Printed in the United States of America.

J I H G F E D C B A

Library of Congress Cataloging-in-Publication Data
is available from the publisher.

This publication is designed to provide accurate and authoritative information with regard to the subject matter covered. It is sold with the understanding that the publisher is not engaged in rendering legal, accounting, or other professional advice. If legal advice or other expert assistance is required, the services of a competent professional person should be sought.

—From a *Declaration of Principles* jointly adopted by a Committee of the American Bar Association and a Committee of Publishers and Associations

Many of the designations used by manufacturers and sellers to distinguish their product are claimed as trademarks. Where those designations appear in this book and Adams Media was aware of a trademark claim, the designations have been printed with initial capital letters.

This book is available at quantity discounts for bulk purchases.
For information, please call 1-800-289-0963.

Acknowledgments

Writing a book is a lot like life. The best are shepherded along with the help of friends and mentors. And so it is with this book. I would be remiss if I didn't mention them and my gratitude for their help.

I am grateful to my collaborator, Curt Schleier, who has worked with me on my most recent manuscripts. He is, of course, an excellent writer and editor, with several books and hundreds of articles to his credit. He is also an excellent trainer; Curt teaches business writing skills to corporate executives and government executives. He knows how to ask the right questions that force me to hone in on the problems and situations we're discussing at the moment. But most important of all, he is extremely simpatico and a pleasure to work with. I'm proud to call him my friend.

It goes almost without saying that I want to thank my editor at Adams, Peter Archer. I'd also like to acknowledge my students. Hundreds of them have stayed in touch, sharing their experiences and ideas with me.

Last—but certainly far from least—this is for Anne, Jennifer, and Danielle, whose support and love keep me going.

Contents

Introduction

From time to time, after a speech or one of my classes, someone will approach me and ask if there is such a thing as a "born salesman." Two things come to mind. First, no one ever asks me in public, during, say, a question-and-answer session. They always approach me privately and almost shyly. It's as though they suspect that the question is silly and that people will laugh at them if they say it out loud in front of a group.

The other thing that comes to mind is my father. My dad sold printing in New York City, at a time when New York was the printing capital of the world. At the time, entire Manhattan neighborhoods were lined with printers. There were big printers who ran off everything from stock certificates and bonds to the entire runs of magazines such as *Life*, *Look*, and the *Saturday Evening Post*. And there were small printers who did letterheads and wedding invitations.

As you can imagine, the competition was fierce—and sometimes even cutthroat. But Dad loved it. Chasing contracts invigorated him, he said. It kept him young. He used to take me into his bedroom and practiced what he called his spiels. He'd asked me what I thought, but what the heck did I know?

The best days were when my father completed a major sale. He'd come home and twirl my mother around the living room, and take us all out to dinner. And as we ate, he'd tell us how he did it, how he convinced his new client that the only place to get his printing was at his company.

His face glowed and his enthusiasm was contagious. More than once people at surrounding tables got involved in our conversation. I distinctly remember once when a man sitting not far from us—someone my father had never met—was so caught up in our excitement, he bought my father a celebratory drink.

There's no question in my mind that I went into sales because of him. And there's no question in my mind that a large part of the success I've had is because of the techniques he taught me.

Selling was different back then. It was largely done by the seat of the salesman's pants. There were no sales techniques. No sales training. Managers figured if you were glib, if you had the gift of gab, you had what it took. Back then, the sales world was filled with Willie Lomans, who glad-handed people into signing contracts.

My father was different. His colleagues called him the general, because he planned his sales effort the way military leaders prepared for battles. I imagine some called him that name sarcastically, as in "There goes the general again on another sales call."

His success I believe in large measure was due to his careful planning, his attention to detail, his almost instinctive understanding that every client was different.

But it was more than that. He had the fire in his belly. He believed in what he was doing. He felt the printing product he sold was of the highest quality and it wasn't so much that he never took no for an answer; it was that he never let a "no" deter him. He kept coming back at prospects with new ideas and new proposals.

So to get back to the question: Is there such an animal as a born salesperson? I believe there is. I can't prove it. I believe there are people—men and women—who are born with the innate skills to sell. You might be one of them. I believe that not everyone is aware of all their inherent potential.

If you are one of those people who were created to sell, this book is for you. The skill set I describe here is based on more than thirty-five years in sales and observing salespeople. It is based on interaction with more than 500,000 students. And if you follow the suggestions listed on the following pages, I believe you will go a long way toward fulfilling your promise.

However, the reality is that there are few "natural" salespeople around, in the same way that there are few Michael Jordans. There are far more elite role players who make it to the show by dint of hard work and practice. Consider Larry Bird: He wasn't a naturally gifted athlete like Jordan, but he worked hard at his game. Even in elementary school, he was the first one at practice and the last one to leave. If everyone shot 100 free throws, he shot 200.

Is there anyone out there who wouldn't like to be Larry Bird? I thought so. So I feel comfortable passing on these "secrets" to you, too. Because using the hints offered on the following pages will make you a better salesperson, too. They can unlock your potential and bring you to new sales heights.

Stephan Schiffman
New York City
February 2009

Chapter

The Born Salesperson

Unless you've just started in the business, you've probably worked with a born salesperson. You know the men or women I mean. They never have a hair out of place, an ounce of fat on their bodies, and never, ever perspire. No matter how hot it is, they just don't sweat. Do you have any idea how annoying that is and they are? Of course you do.

Everything comes easily for them. They make a cold call and the lead not only picks up the phone, but invites them over for lunch. First meetings lead to presentations. Presentations lead to contracts. And contracts lead to commissions and bonuses and company-paid trips for the family to Oahu.

Meanwhile, we're slaving away and sweating for half the results. We can't help but be jealous. Jealous? I wasn't really jealous; I just hated them. Yet I wanted to be one of them.

Who Are These People?

Usually when people talk about someone with natural ability they refer to an athlete, mostly because a great athlete's gifts are often very visible and very obvious. Michael Jordan is the example I most frequently use. I still vividly remember watching him (against my beloved Knicks) shift the ball from hand to hand in mid air to avoid a defender and then dunk. You see the same thing at times with great running backs who change direction quicker than you or I (well, certainly I) can even spot a hole, let alone will our legs to move. Jordan had a gift and knew it from the time he was a child. Michael Jordan was born to play basketball.

Athletes aren't the only ones with innate abilities. Consider some top-ranked concert musicians, for example. Arthur Rubenstein, Isaac Stern, and Vladimir Horowitz were child prodigies. I took piano lessons for about five years from the time I was about six until I couldn't stand it anymore—and my parents couldn't stand my griping. Beethoven and Mozart composed music before they were in their teens.

Innate abilities like this, whether you want to call them genetic gifts or gifts from a higher power, are not limited to people with glamorous jobs. I had a carpenter come to my house once and just based on my verbal description he was able to oversee a major addition to a vacation house. He didn't need blueprints. He was able to see what I wanted in his head as I described it to him.

I happen to live in New York City and as I walk around the city I'll periodically see police officers who have lines of medals and awards running from their badges up to their shoulder. The chances are these are cops who have noses for crime. Something just ticks inside them when they see something you or I likely will just pass by, but they know is out of the ordinary.

Innate Skill Is Not Enough

Natural borns are, as the name implies, born and not made. They have a specific skill or skills but that is not enough. They also have to recognize that they have this skill and have the opportunity to put it to use. To give a far-fetched example, a person born with the innate skills to be a carpenter will probably never understand the gift he has if he's raised in the far north or south, in climates where there are few trees and wood is not always the building block of choice.

The carpenter who worked on my house, on the other hand, started woodworking with his father before he hit his teens. He loved it and, unlike me and the piano, never had to be dragged to the lathe or whatever other machines young carpentry prodigies use. I'm sure Michael Jordan shot hoops every night until the sun went down. He shot (what we used to call) set shots and drove to the basket and put up free throw after free throw until he couldn't raise his arm over his head anymore.

This brings us back to the born salesman. He was probably a leader among his friends. He was (and remains) glib and quick-witted. Based on my experience with born salesmen, they all read a lot—on many subjects. They can talk about almost everything. And people like them and gravitate toward them.

In short, they're pretty much everything I wasn't as a kid.

What, you say? You? Let me make something perfectly clear here at the outset. Despite what you may assume:

I am not a born salesman.

Everything that follows in this book is written from that perspective.

That doesn't mean I haven't been successful in my career. Clearly I have. I made a lot of money pounding the pavement and then I made more training others to make a lot of money, too. And I made even more moolah writing about some of the techniques I've developed.

But I repeat, because this is important: **I am not a born salesman.**

Whatever I've accomplished, I've achieved because I worked hard at it. I kept my eyes and my mind open. And I learned. First I learned from my old man, one of the most gifted salesmen I've ever met. Then I learned from watching coworkers and even one or two sales managers.

"Open" is the key word in the last paragraph. If I saw something that seemed to work, I was more than willing to try it. And if it didn't work for me the first time around, I didn't immediately discard it. I figured if it worked for John or Ed at the next desk, it could work for me. I'd just have to modify the technique to fit me.

I kept what worked, discarded what didn't. I refined my techniques. I worked harder. And I sold.

So can you. I'm not the smartest guy in the world. I'm not the most ambitious. I'm not a guy who spends eighty hours a week working. If I found a way to boost my sales, so can you. That's what this book is about: Just because you don't have the natural disposition of a born salesperson doesn't mean you can't achieve that level of success. I did.

I did like Mike. I broke down different elements of the sales process and worked on them individually. I analyzed my game and figured out what were my strengths—I'm a reasonably well-spoken person—and my weaknesses—presentations. I worked on my weaknesses until I was less weak and eventually stronger.

And I became relentless.

Those of us who are not born salespeople don't have the luxury of being casual about what we do. We have to keep at it and at it and at it until it becomes ingrained in us. And even then we have to keep going, or we'll lose that muscle memory.

Over the next couple of dozen chapters I am going to be a coach. Just as a coach shows his players films of their games and breaks them down to study offense, defense, and so forth, I am going to break down the born salesperson game film into its various components. Then I am going to come up with a game plan for you to show how you can approximate what the born salesperson does.

It will take work. What comes effortlessly for the born sales reps requires effort from people like me and probably you. But my experience has been that if you expend the effort, if you walk the extra mile, you will be rewarded. Your commissions will increase. Your recognition in your field will increase. And so will your sense of satisfaction.

Hey, you've been with me this far. Just read on.

WHAT TO TAKE FROM THIS CHAPTER

1. Yes, there are people who are naturally gifted sales reps. No matter to what you ascribe this ability—whether it is genetic or an award from a higher power, there are folks for whom the sales process is as ordinary as breathing is to you and me.

2. Even the "natural borns" have to recognize these skills and put themselves in a position to use them.

3. This doesn't mean that the rest of us are doomed to a life in sales purgatory. It just means we have to be more conscious of the sales process, more deliberate as we go through the steps from cold calling to closing, more mindful of what we do.

4. We have to be open to new ideas and approaches, willing to at least try things outside our comfort zones.

Chapter 2

Give Me Some Attitude

Early in my career I worked for a company that had AIM as its sales motto. AIM was an acronym for Attitude Is Money. I never liked the slogan, but I came to understand the thinking behind it. I was a young salesman at a time when young salespeople were typically thrown into the water. Either you taught yourself how to swim among the sharks or they ate you alive. Either way, there was some resolution. You survived or you didn't.

And as I looked around for some kind of life preserver to keep me afloat until I started closing sales more consistently, I noticed something about the people who seemed to close a sale every time they left the office. Even then I referred to them (privately, in my mind) as born salesmen (they were all men then); and as I studied what they did and how they did it, I noticed they all had something in common. It was their positive attitude.

These born salespeople seemed to have it all. Physically, they always looked great—as though they just got back from Aspen or the Turks and Caicos. Their clothing seemed hand tailored, their smiles always bright, their complexions clear.

Mentally, too, they always seemed on top of their game. They were well spoken, quick-witted, and could converse intelligently about almost anything.

They acted as though they had been winners all their lives—and no one doubted them. From my perspective, they were the BMOCs—Big

Men on Campus—the same guys I always detested when I was in college. The student government president. The quarterback. The rich kid with the shiny new Corvette. They approached everything they did with vigor and confidence; they believed they could accomplish anything they set their mind to. There was no question that they were going to close that sale. And the next sale. And the one after that.

That rubbed off on their customers. These salespeople were so sure of themselves that clients figured (or so it seemed to me), "Why swim against the tide? It's easier to just place the order."

How was I supposed to compete against that?

Like a Bolt of Lightning

I really didn't have a clue. I only hoped to keep my head above water until I could figure it out. The realization came to me about eight months into the job. I'd developed a "great relationship" with a prospect—we'll call him Joe at Company A. We'd gotten to a point where we were really comfortable with each other. I'd make a proposal and he'd say no. I'd make another proposal and he'd say no. It was like a play in which we both knew our parts.

But that all changed one day when I was on my way to work. I'm not going to give you specifics, because details don't matter. Suffice it to say that I was sitting on the subway reading a trade magazine about our industry. That day, the paper happened to run a profile of Company A's president. In the story he revealed that the firm was in the early design stages of developing a new product. He went on to briefly describe what he had in mind, and the impact it would have on the market and his company.

And it suddenly hit me. I don't know where it came from but it was literally like a bolt out of the blue. My company made something that could—would—make Company A's new product line a success.

When I got to my stop I rushed out of the subway and up the steps. And this I remember with clarity, as though it happened yesterday not almost four decades ago. I didn't stop in the coffee shop for my black coffee and a bagel, as was my custom. There was no time. I rushed to my desk, grabbed my calculator, and set to work. I figured out a variety of pricing schemes in what seemed like minutes, but must have been a couple of hours.

I immediately called Joe and told him something had come up and it was urgent that I see him that day. At first he asked me if everything was okay. I told him, no, not everything was okay, everything was great. And I'd tell him all about it. He just had to see me today.

He said he'd squeeze me in at 2:30, but couldn't give me much time. He had a 2:45. But he wasn't talking to the old Stephan Schiffman, the one who calmly took his no as a final answer. I knew that once I got into his office I wasn't leaving until I was done—and I wasn't done until I had an order.

I got to Company A at 2 P.M. Joe was in his office when the reception-ist called to let him know I was there. Normally he had no qualms about keeping me waiting. But I guess curiosity about why I was suddenly so excited and insistent got the best of him. He came out and brought me back to his office immediately. "Okay," he asked, "what was so important I had to see you today?"

I told him about what I read in the trade paper. I told him about the ideas I came up with. I told him about the pricing plan and delivery schedule I'd created. And I sat back waiting for—this time—a positive response.

All the time I'd been talking, Joe looked at me quizzically. I assumed it was because he was trying to figure out what had caused this unex-pected transformation in my selling style. The person who was making this presentation was different from the Stephan Schiffman he'd been used to dealing with. But that turned out only to be partly the case.

He of course knew about the new project, but was unaware that news of it had been released. As I found out later, the company president had revealed the news about this significant new project prematurely, and that's what threw Joe for a loop. After my presentation, Joe asked me to hang around. He went out and after about ten minutes returned with his boss, a senior VP type who had purchasing responsibility.

The Right Product at the Right Time

Joe had told him what I'd said, but he asked me to repeat it as he took notes. "I have to be honest," he said to me. "But I don't think anybody here thought of that." (By "that" he meant using my product in the manner I'd suggested.) "Would you mind coming back tomorrow and making a full presentation to the committee that's shepherding this project? I realize it's short notice, but we're in a little bit of a time bind."

Would I mind? Does night follow day? Of course I'd be happy to come back. I spent the rest of the day preparing a presentation. Remember, this was before laptops and PowerPoint presentations. I typed everything up, made Xerox copies, and was ready the next morning with what today would be considered a rudimentary presentation. But the folks at Company A loved it.

Their order alone catapulted me to the top sales spot in my company. I was number one, and when I stopped to think about it, here's why I think it happened.

Two things happened simultaneously. First, I had a product one of my customers needed and I was able to offer it at a price point and at a delivery schedule that worked for everyone. But it was just as important that I knew it, and because of that my attitude—and my approach—changed. I became enthusiastic and that enthusiasm spread. I was the same person, but I wasn't. My prospect, Joe, may not have known what it was, but he sensed something was different. And that made him different in the way he reacted to me.

He wouldn't have made time for the old Schiffman, but this new guy, he had to put him on the appointment schedule. It was like a high. I knew nothing could touch me. I was the man. For the first time, I understood the way my father felt after he closed a big sale. I was, for this one brief moment, a born salesman.

If you've been in the business for any length of time you've almost certainly had moments like this, where everything comes together as though the patron saint of sales decided to make you his pet project. And for you newcomers, it is an unbelievable feeling.

Positive vibes seem to emanate from born salespeople all the time. And that enthusiasm perpetuates both sales and enthusiasm. For born salespeople, it becomes the opposite of a vicious cycle, a kind of self-fulfilling prophecy that leads to higher and higher commissions and bigger and bigger smiles.

What about the rest of us? How do we keep smiling under the pressures of the job and life? There are a bunch of things we can do as discussed in the next chapter. But really the first step is to understand the importance of projecting what Brian Wilson calls good vibrations. If you come to a sales call with a defeatist attitude, you will be defeated. It's as simple as that.

And if worse comes to worst, remember that old standby: The secret of success is sincerity. Once you can fake that, you've got it made. And the same can be said about enthusiasm.

I didn't make that up, although I wish I did. Credit goes to Jean Giraudoux, a French diplomat and novelist, who also was famous for saying, "only the mediocre are always at their very best."

He was, of course right—on both counts.

WHAT TO TAKE FROM THIS CHAPTER

1. There are a lot of different elements to a successful sale, but among the most important is attitude.
2. The way you present yourself—your posture, your clothing, your tone, even the way you look at a customer—gives off subtle signals.
3. If you act like a loser—slumped over, not looking your prospect straight in the eyes—you come across negatively and people react to you negatively.
4. Conversely, if you come in with a can-do attitude and confidence, prospects will react more positively toward you.

Chapter  3

Creating Attitude (Part I)

In the first chapter, I told you that I'm not a born salesman. I had to work—and work hard—to achieve whatever measure of success I've enjoyed. In fact, I didn't enjoy any measure of success until I changed my attitude, until everything fell into place and I had that one can't-miss sale.

I was still the same guy I was before that fateful subway ride. Nothing but my attitude had changed. But by simply approaching my client in a more positive manner, I altered the entire dynamic of our relationship. Previously my "client," Joe, listened to what I had to say, but I never had the impression that he heard me. The only difference between this sales call and all the other times I'd visited him was that the positive energy of my newfound enthusiasm infected him, as well. And for the first time he genuinely paid attention to my message.

I'm not a fool. I know that if I didn't have a real opportunity for Joe and Company A, he would not have purchased anything from me. But I also believe that if the old Stephan Schiffman had made the identical proposal, he wouldn't have been heard. Joe would have told me what he always told me: "I'll let you know."

An Enthusiasm Implant

In this chapter, I offer another pertinent confession: I am not Dr. Phil. Heck, I'm not even Oprah. My point is that I don't have a magic pill that will turn you into an enthusiastic salesperson who wows every client. I don't know how to create a positive aura around you. As near as I can tell, there aren't any miracle cures. There are no attitude implants available.

But is it possible to imbue yourself with this winner's attitude? I say yes. And, frankly, the easiest way to become a winner is also the most obvious: win. And win consistently. A positive attitude breeds success. Success breeds success. Success breeds a positive attitude. It's an unvicious cycle.

I knew I was going to land the Company A account and I knew it was going to be big. My first impulse after the contract was signed was to relax. What a feeling! I'd just made my numbers for the entire year with one sale. I spoke to my new bride about taking a vacation; a couple of weeks in Europe seemed like an appropriate reward. But she had a new job and couldn't get time off; so I went back to work.

It was the best thing that could have happened to me. I was still riding a high from Company A, and it carried over into the project I had on my desk. When I made cold calls in the morning, my percentage of appointments tripled. Not only did people agree to see me, they seemed anxious to do so.

I'm sure there's some deep, logical psychological explanation for this, but I chalk it up to something very simple: People like to be with winners. You see how celebrities always have entourages around them? It's the same principle. People believe that the winning will rub off on them.

I can't explain it; all I know is that my numbers shot up. And as long as I maintained a winning attitude they stayed up. I wasn't able to maintain the winning attitude indefinitely; we all have slumps. But as long as I had the winning attitude I did very well.

Of course, telling you to be positive is one thing; getting you to be positive is quite another. But the reality is that just buying this book is the first step. It indicates to me that you want to improve your sales situation, and wanting success is the first step.

If you've been in the business for a while, the chances are that at one point in your career, you've had a sales epiphany similar to the one I had. Remind yourself what that was like, visualize that success, and see if that will carry you over.

Build blocks. I was very lucky in that when my epiphany happened I landed a major account. But that was the exception to the rule. Early on, aim for something that is easily achievable. Something as simple as getting a long-time customer to increase their order or the items they purchase from your company.

Do that just a few times and your numbers will start to grow; before long people will start to notice. And if you didn't do so before, once your colleagues and bosses start viewing you as a winner, you will see yourself in the same way. Then your entire approach to your job will change. Success breeds success. Yes, I know I said that before. I'm just trying to emphasize the point.

Ironically, the day I wrote this chapter I had a lengthy conversation with the vice president of sales for a major real estate company. One of the subjects that we discussed was the role of incentives as motivators versus say a cash bonus or a higher commission. He said in his experience, most salespeople would rather win, say, a large, flat-screen high-definition TV than get comparable cash—or even more cash. The recognition that comes with the television is far more valuable to most salespeople than the equivalent amount of cash.

Why? You put cash in your pocket, spend it, and it's gone. But the TV is a tangible symbol of a salesperson's success. When you throw a Super Bowl party—because of course everyone wants to see the game on your giant TV—what is to prevent you from telling your guests exactly how the TV came to be in your den? You won it because you're excellent at what you do!

The not-so-original conclusion the real estate executive and I came up with is that the best salespeople are competitive and very little motivates them like winning and the recognition that comes with that.

I've saved my hokiest suggestion for last. It's an idea I credit to my lack of athletic ability. Remember what we said early on in this book. The difference between a "natural born" and you or me is that for the gifted one everything comes naturally. They don't have to think about it. When it comes to sales, they seem to have a natural gift of gab and get along with everyone.

The same holds true with athletic ability. Not that Michael Jordan didn't practice; I'm sure he did. But he was able to do things instinctively on the court that others could only dream about, things that couldn't be taught or practiced.

I'm not a big basketball player, but there was a time that I played tennis regularly. Not well, but regularly. Two or three mornings a week in the summer I'd meet Bob, a teacher friend of mine, early in the morning and we'd play a couple of sets before I went home to get ready for work.

Compared to me Bob was Roger Federer. But I didn't mind losing because I enjoyed the competition. (That's a lie. I hated losing and broke more than one racquet while expressing my displeasure.) I started taking tennis lessons. In each class, the pro would concentrate on a different aspect of my game: my stance or my grip or my serve or my net play. And when we practiced (with the pro of course hitting the ball right at me) I was pretty good. But the next day, when I played with Bob it was just me again.

And every time I lost by a large margin (6-0, 6-0 was a typical score) I'd analyze what I did wrong. I didn't prepare my stroke properly. I didn't switch grips in time. I didn't bend my knees. And the next day I'd go out and make the same mistakes again.

So it occurred to me that I wasn't preparing properly. What Bob did naturally, I had to think about, and thinking took time. So I decided to prepare. I made notes about each of the things I did wrong and put them on top of my tennis bag. And before I left for the court the following morning, I studied where I needed improvement. And when

I got on the court and started to play I was ready to beat his sorry behind.

I didn't. Let's not go crazy. But the scores changed from 6-0, 6-0 to 6-3 and 6-4. The games became far more competitive, and we both had more fun. And I broke fewer racquets.

Eventually I decided this technique ought to work in the business world, too. So I left notes around my office reminding me how important a positive attitude was. I put a Post-it on the mirror in my bathroom so I would see it when I went to shower and shave. I put it on my Mr. Coffee.

Believe me I'm not one for those inspirational posters you see on the walls of a lot of offices. Like I said, I know this leave-yourself-a-note-deal comes off sounding hokey. But—and it's a big but—the bottom line is that a positive attitude will make a significant difference in your life. How can it hurt to remind yourself of that at every turn?

WHAT TO TAKE FROM THIS CHAPTER

1. You can't tell yourself you want to be confident and—boom—you are. It doesn't work that way.

2. The first step is to remind yourself how important confidence can be to your career—your life really. Try leaving notes around, prompts that will help you start off each morning on the right foot. I taped a note to my shaving mirror where I can't miss it. I put another by the coffee pot. And then a third at my desk. After a while, confidence became a habit. And I didn't need reminders. Confidence became second nature.

3. I got lucky. I gained confidence and scored a big sale almost immediately. Mostly it doesn't happen that way. Set realistic goals: Five successful cold calls a week; two appointments with new customers a week. Success—even a small success—builds confidence.

Chapter

The Right Attitude (Part II) Means the Right Look

The interesting thing about natural-born salespeople is that they *seem* to live a life unblemished by trouble. They *seem* to feed off this positive energy and give off a positive aura that breeds success.

The key word in that paragraph is "seem." The truth of the matter is that no one goes through life without some difficulties, including the naturally gifted. Consider the following:

I met a guy, let's call him Bill, when we were paired as part of a foursome in a golf tournament at a large convention. I liked him immediately because he was so good at the game that he carried me. In fact, his handicap was me. I don't want to say I'm bad at golf, only because "bad" is far too kind a description of my game. But, thanks to Bill and for the first time in my life, I won a golf trophy.

So of course we went to the nineteenth hole to celebrate, and got to talking. He was a very successful salesman. In fact, although I didn't realize it when we first met on the course, I had heard of him and his triumphs.

Not only was Bill an almost legendary success at what he did, but he looked the part, too. His clothes fit perfectly yet he had a casual, care-free look about him, as though he'd just thrown on whatever was in his closet. (I say that by way of contrast to people we all know—men and women—who spend hours trying to put together just the right outfit to make them look casual.)

Bill was so perfect he would have been easy to hate, but I couldn't do it. He was also extremely nice. (And of course he won me the trophy.) Speaking to him over a round of drinks was like speaking to an old friend. It was as though we shared a lifetime of experiences. He seemed genuinely pleased when he found I was involved in sales training, and we shared anecdotes through several rounds of, uh, refreshments.

As afternoon faded into evening, Bill pulled his chair a little closer to mine and asked if he could confide in me. He had a persistent fear of failure and wanted to know if I had any trick for overcoming this phobia.

I was surprised—no shocked—by what he said—and quite frankly that he even said it to me. I guess he could tell what I was thinking from the look on my face. "I know it doesn't make any sense," he said. "But I cannot begin to tell you the anxiety I feel every time I meet a prospect for the first time or whenever I make a presentation. And I've been keeping it inside so long I feel like it's going to eat me up." He quickly apologized, adding he shouldn't have burdened me with his problem. Then he chuckled and said he probably also shouldn't have had those last two drinks.

I was incredulous. I thought about it for a few minutes and then told him the only way I could help him is if he answered a question for me: How did he do it? How did he cover up his greatest fears? I told him: "I don't think you have a problem. I actually consider what you do a significant achievement. Most people who feel the way you do would walk away from the job, not confront their fears."

At first Bill didn't know what to make of my response. We both sipped our beverages in silence for a couple of minutes. And then he looked up and smiled at me. "You know, no one ever put it that way before. I should have met you fifteen years ago." Then he added: "I really don't know what I do. It's nothing conscious. I just reach a point of no return and sort of understand that I have to tough things out."

That conversation took place some time ago but stayed with me. If Bill is typical, even natural salespeople have chinks in their armor. The difference between them and the rest of us is twofold: First, they find a way to tough it out. Second, and more important, they don't let the chinks show. Until he told me about it, I never would have guessed that there was anything wrong in Bill's life.

I'd seen this before. However, my discussion with Bill crystallized for me some things that had been swirling around in my mind but I hadn't been able to put my finger on. In fact, it turned out to be one of the main reasons I decided to write this book.

Everyone has imperfections. The most important secret of a natural-born salesperson is that he overcomes these flaws and doesn't let them show. If everyone is flawed in some way, why can't we all overcome our imperfections?

Of course, it isn't as easy as that. My conversation with Bill didn't automatically calm his fears. We've kept in touch, of course, and his boots still quake before an appointment. But he says he has a better perspective on his fears now, and that's made the process easier for him.

It's the same for the rest of us. We may not be able to eliminate all our flaws, but we can work toward that goal, get rid of some, and get a better perspective on others. And if we do that, we'll be better salespeople.

Create the Right Look

Some of the changes we have to make may be difficult. But the more I thought about it, the more I realized that there are some very simple things any salesperson can do to start the ball rolling, to create that aura of invincibility. Consider this:

There is a saying that the clothes make the man (and woman). It's true. You only have one shot at making a good first impression. I've had a salesman come into my office with his jacket off, his shirtsleeves rolled up, and the perspiration running down his face. It was a hot and very humid New York City summer afternoon, and maybe he thought that excused his disheveled appearance. But there was and is no excuse. If you want to be treated like a professional, you have to look like one.

I make it a point to try to show up at least 15 minutes early for every appointment and use the restroom mirror to check my look. I want to be spotless when a potential customer sees me. I make sure my tie is in place, my hair combed, and my suit neatly pressed.

There's something else I've done from early on in my sales career. I've always had a presentation suit. When I was a young man, I used to buy my suits at a chain of stores called Robert Hall. I don't know if it was a national chain or just regional in the New York City area, but I vividly remember paying $25 or $30 for perfectly adequate suits.

But once a year back then I splurged. I went to Brooks Brothers and paid about $150 for an expensive suit, plus another thirty or forty bucks for a dress shirt and silk tie. I saved that suit for special occasions such as important presentations. That suit changed me in a way I can't explain. But it made me feel better about myself. It gave me confidence.

The closest analogy I can make is what in major league baseball is called Yankee pride. They say when ball players come to the Bronx and put on the pinstripe uniform they almost feel the tradition of pennants and World Series wins. It was kind of like that with my presentation suit. I felt I could belt every pitch out of the ballpark. I stood a little taller whenever I wore it.

That brings up something that's a little delicate. If you are dramatically overweight, you have to get yourself in shape. Like the suit, you will feel better about yourself. And people will look at you differently. There has been study after study about this subject, and most people surveyed say they have negative feelings toward obese people. They feel they don't have any self control and are not trustworthy.

I know it's not politically correct, but if you are seriously overweight you probably don't need me to tell you what the ramifications of that are; you've lived with them. It's no secret that pretty much everyone I consider a natural salesperson is in pretty good shape. That doesn't mean guys have to have a six-pack; but it does mean they shouldn't be carrying around a basketball. The same is true for the ladies. I certainly don't want to hurt anyone's feelings, but I'd be less than honest with you if I didn't mention this.

If I may quote the great Fernando from *Saturday Night Live*: "It is better to look good than feel good, and, dahling, you look mah-vel-us."

Enough said?

Feeling Like a Winner Inside

In addition to being in good shape outside, every natural-born salesperson I've ever met works out inside, too. They tend to be voracious readers of newspapers, magazines, and books. In fact, if there is one overriding suggestion I make in this book it is to read.

Reading does a lot of things for you. We call what we do sales, but we are really in the communications business. We have to communicate to our customers and potential customers the value of the products we sell. And reading does so much to make you a better salesperson.

First of all, it improves your vocabulary. It also increases your understanding of proper grammar and the way words are used. It improves your writing and speaking. And that happens pretty much no matter what you read: mysteries, romance, science fiction, sports books—it doesn't make a difference.

Frankly, whenever I interview someone for a job, I ask what books they've read lately. It's not the only thing I base a hiring decision on, but it is a key element in the process.

There's another benefit to reading. Not only will you be a better, more eloquent speaker, but you will also have more to talk about. One of the things that natural borns do extremely well is to create a conversation around a sale. And the more well-read you are, the more you'll have to converse about.

And in the same way that you only have one opportunity to make a physical impression, you also only have one good shot at making a mental connection. The ability to speak knowledgeably on a variety of subjects makes you seem multidimensional and more interesting. I don't only mean upper-crust literary subjects, but pop culture, too.

There are three major New York City newspapers and I read one (the *New York Times*) and skim the other two every day. I read the movie reviews and the box scores. I pretty much know the standings of every New York area team in every major sport. If there's a hot show on TV, I watch it whether I like it or not. (I loved the *Sopranos*, hated *Sex and the City*, but watched both religiously.)

The point is that the better prepared you are in every facet of your game, the more confident you'll be. And the more confident you are, the more you send out a positive aura. And the more you send out a positive aura . . . well you get the point.

WHAT TO TAKE FROM THIS CHAPTER

1. The right attitude is not just mental, it's physical, too.

2. If you're not well dressed it will reflect upon you in the same manner as lack of confidence. Given a choice, people want to deal with someone who projects positive vibes.

3. This is your livelihood. Invest in it. Get yourself a couple of really good suits, expensive shirts, and silk ties. Your customers will notice—and so will you. You will feel better about yourself when you look in the mirror.

4. Get back to your fighting weight. You can look in the mirror and tell yourself the problem is in your genes. But if you can't fit into your jeans, it doesn't make a difference why. If you are over-weight, you come across as a person who lacks self-control and can't be trusted.

5. If you walk away from this book with one lesson, it is that reading is one of the most important things you can do. It improves your vocabulary, improves your grammar, it improves your understanding of American idioms—that is the way words are used. Reading will improve your communications skills. It will make you a better writer and a better speaker. Ironically, these benefits come no matter what you read—even mysteries or science fiction.

6. However, reading newspapers and news magazines has an added benefit; they make you a better conversationalist. You will be better informed about what's going on in the world and come across more intelligently and positively.

Creating an Environment for Success

The environment we create for ourselves impacts our ability to succeed. I know I'm stating the obvious, yet sometimes all of us demonstrate an uncanny ability to not see the forest because of the trees.

The simplest example I can offer relates to what I said in the previous chapter about getting into shape because the physical image you present impacts your ability to sell. Let's say you are trying to lose twenty pounds. Keeping your refrigerator stocked with ice cream, soda, and cake is probably not the best way to create a good weight-loss environment.

And it isn't just a matter of what you do. You have to surround yourself with people who are supportive. Suppose that cake in the fridge isn't for you, but for your spouse or roommate instead. Suppose you go out with friends who urge you to take another slice of pizza. Obviously, if the people who surround you aren't supportive, it greatly diminishes your chances for success.

And that's what I mean about creating an environment to succeed.

For example, I know a guy, let's call him Robert, who for the last twenty-five years has been one of the most successful commercial insurance agents in the business. He has top *Fortune* 500 clients, wins sales awards every year, and can now easily afford the sumptuous lifestyle he leads. It wasn't until I got to know him better that I discovered it wasn't always this way.

Fresh out of college, he joined the family business, where things went badly—through no fault of his own. The biggest problem was that his father wasn't as prepared to give up management and control of the company as he'd promised Robert. There followed a series of moves to different sales jobs in different industries and different states. It wasn't until he joined his current company that he had any success at all. And once he tasted that sweet fruit, he couldn't get enough of it.

What was different? A number of things. What follows are some of the things he told me that changed in his life as well as others I've picked up over the years.

Find a Product You Believe In

There is no worse feeling than going in to work every day knowing that you are going to have to spend eight hours lying to people. Oh, yes, this product has a great safety record. Of course, service is never a problem. We guarantee everything for five years (except—very quietly—all that stuff in the tiny print). It is demoralizing. It is dehumanizing. And it wears on you. This is not about selling the number one or two products in the field. It is about looking at yourself in the mirror every morning and not turning away in disgust. This is critical. You want to work for a company that is proud of what it does and is willing to stand by it.

Find a Company That Helps You Succeed

Over the course of his pre-insurance years, Robert sold for (varying lengths of time) perhaps eight companies. But only one provided him with accouterments to actually help him sell. At most of his jobs, he was handed sales promotion material that looked as though it was created by a five-year-old in need of a nap. I know I've worked for companies like that. Rather than spend a few extra dollars and get sales literature professionally designed and written, these company execs "create" something on their computers, print it out, and then hope it will do the job.

In the last chapter I spoke a little about the fact that you have only one opportunity to make a first impression. Well, the same thing holds true for your company. If you hand shoddy-looking sales literature to a potential client, what is he or she supposed to think? That your product is any better? You want whatever you mail out or leave behind to reflect the quality of your product or service and your pride and commitment. Anything less is a disservice to you. (At this point, I don't even care about that company.)

Find a Company That Doesn't Play Games

Have you ever flown on a business trip and been seated next to a couple on vacation who paid 25 percent of what you did? It may not have annoyed you if you have a big company paying for the ticket. But I have a little company paying for my tickets and *I own it*. So you can imagine how annoyed I get.

But at least airline ticket prices are published. If I was in a position to buy them fourteen days in advance and stay over a Saturday night, I could have the tickets for the same price the vacationing couple paid. But what happens when you work for a company that cuts deals just to clinch a sale? Certainly your sales numbers will increase momentarily. But, believe me, it's only a Pyrrhic victory. For one thing, cutting deals ultimately erodes the bottom line. If you cut prices for one customer by, say, 10 percent, where will that 10 percent come from? From profits, of course.

Ultimately, your other customers will find out about the cut-rate deal afforded to a competitor, and they will be annoyed too. They may take their business elsewhere. They may insist on the same deal. I don't know what they will do—except for one thing: Your contacts there are never likely to trust you again.

Again I state the obvious. You're not in the business of selling a product or service. You're in the business of building a relationship. And if you don't have trust, you have nothing.

Become Part of a Team

We have all worked at companies that were rife with petty jealousies. Instead of encouraging us, coworkers were jealous of every sale we made. That kind of attitude isn't generated on its own. It is a reflection of management's attitude, particularly the sales manager.

The worst job I ever had was working for a guy who took pleasure in wielding power. He'd say one thing one day, and another the next. He'd okay an expenditure and then deny it. He'd call mandatory meetings when I had outside appointments. And he was a yeller. The entire office could hear him yelling when he was ticked off at one of his salespeople. Clearly, that wasn't conducive to good morale.

The turnover rate was extremely high. (In fact, we used to kid that the company alumni would meet every December 7 aboard the *USS Arizona*.) Anyway, selling isn't easy. Sometimes you have to bust your chops to get a sale, or work long hours. And for those of us who are road warriors, it means spending considerable time away from your family. You don't want to do it if you're working for someone who is a rotten son of a, eh, gun.

You want to work for someone who will help you clinch a sale, not get in your way. Someone who happily credits you for your hard work instead of grabbing all the glory for him- (or her-) self. You want to work with someone who will add value to what you do, sit with you while you rehearse a presentation, make constructive suggestions that make it better. In short, you want someone who will pat you on the back, not kick you in the ...

Find a Company That Appreciates Your Hard Work

I don't know of any company that doesn't have some kind of incentive program for its salespeople. But that's just de rigueur (if I can show off my French a little bit). The great companies single out their best salespeople for special recognition. I don't mean just special gift awards—trips or flat-panel HDTVs. They call them up at sales meetings to receive plaques and applause from their peers. It's inexpensive—how much can a plaque cost?—but it shows that the company cares. And, inevitably, that's appreciated by the salesperson.

At this point, you're saying, "Enough of your fairytales, Steve. There is no such company. There is no such job."

Well, you're wrong. Robert found one. And I did. So they definitely are out there. Sure, they're rare. But that doesn't mean you shouldn't try to land one of them. At the very least, you ought to be aware what a perfect job could be like. Then you can strive to make your present job closer to the ideal—or switch to one that is. Frankly, once you do find yourself in a better situation, you'll see how swiftly your attitude improves and, with that, your sales numbers.

WHAT TO TAKE FROM THIS CHAPTER

1. The most important factor in creating the right environment for success is to find a place where you can be happy. It isn't easy, and the chances that you'll find the perfect situation are somewhere between slim and none. But that doesn't mean you shouldn't try to at least get as close as possible.

2. There are a number of different ways to define happiness. It's something you'll have to decide for yourself. And remember, too, that the definition changes as you do, as you get older, presumably wiser, and more comfortable with yourself.

3. One thing doesn't change and that is you must find a product you believe in. Everything else you want in a job can be there for you, but selling something you don't believe in, lying to customers every day, will just wear you down.

4. Working for a company and a boss that appreciates your efforts, wants to help, and rewards you properly—if you find all that give me a call. I want to work there. Just kidding. That kind of job must exist somewhere. But just finding some of these attributes helps create the environment you need to sell and sell well.

Chapter

Following Robert Browning's Advice, or Finding Your "Ness"

I know others have said this before, but the following sentiment is well worth repeating:

The happier you are, the more likely you are to find success.

I consider that to be a basic truth about the world of business—though not everyone agrees with me. Some folks say it the other way: The more successful you are, the happier you will be. But I don't believe that is true. I have never known a sad, bitter person to find success. And even when they've found brief moments to cheer about, it didn't make them happy. So, for me anyway, it's not a chicken-and-egg question: Happiness leads to success, not the other way around.

As I believe we've established, natural-born salespeople carry a positive aura with them, a belief that they are bound to succeed. I believe that they are able to do that because they don't have outside issues distracting them. There are, for want of a better expression, no negative vibes to keep them from focusing on the issues at hand.

How do you find this sense of contentment? I'm glad you asked.

Keeping Work Goals Realistic

British poet Robert Browning wrote, "Ah, but a man's reach should exceed his grasp, or what's a heaven for?"

I am not a big poetry buff, but I must admit that this is a line—one of the few lines, in fact—that stayed with me from high school English classes. What Browning meant was that dreams and ambition are good things. If you aim too low, never shooting for the top in life, then you really haven't lived well. I assume he was talking about man's capacity to become a good person. I took it to be about man's capacity to become a good salesperson. (It's a minor difference hardly worth mentioning, except that in being honest I become a better person.)

Anyway, that line sort of became my motto. As I've said previously here and elsewhere, I was never what you'd call a natural salesman. But I had the gift of gab and desire, and that pretty much drove what successes I've had. I was always a dreamer, a Walter Mitty if you will, looking for a larger apartment, a vacation home, and big bucks. It worked for me.

But about fifteen years ago, I began to notice that students who were a lot like me, dreamers with their futures all mapped out, began incurring unexpected problems in selling. The problem as I found out later was that these people—they tended to be in their late thirties and early forties—weren't happy. And their lack of cheer began to impact their sales.

I suppose this problem has been around for a long time and I was just slow to recognize it. But once I realized that this was a problem, it didn't take me more than a few minutes to spot the students in my class who suffered from what I came to call "Over Ambition Complex" (OAC).

So what I'd do is approach them individually and ask them to join me for coffee or drinks after class. We'd start to talk about their situation, and inevitably the problem was, as my mother used to say after I asked for another piece of cake and then couldn't finish it: "Your eyes are too big for your stomach."

What I was able to discern over a period of two or three years was that all these salespeople were reasonably successful in their early years in the field, but that their goals shifted. I don't want to generalize, because this was hardly a scientific survey. Still, based on my observations, what happened gradually is that their focus switched from selling to acquiring. Perhaps spoiled by their early wins or pushed by overly ambitious spouses, their goals became McMansions and expensive Italian sports cars instead of getting to the next step in the sales process and closing the sale.

Focused on their own needs rather than the customers', they started pressing harder and harder to clinch a sale. Their attitude changed. They became desperate, trying to meet higher mortgage and car payments. And it showed in their work.

Clearly, it is frustrating when your reach consistently exceeds your grasp by a wide and widening margin. If you overextend your goals, if your reach exceeds your grasp by an unattainable amount, then you leave yourself open to the kind of frustration that kills any chance you have for success on any level. So, clearly, your goals have to be realistic. Aiming for and achieving a smaller percentage increase in sales seems to me a lot better than aiming higher and missing.

Remember, sales goals—all your goals, for that matter—are not static. They change, so it makes more sense (as noted in the last chapter) to keep goals realistic and overachieve than to set otherworldly goals and become frustrated by failure. Over achievement equals a happy, positive attitude. Under achievement equals Oscar the Grouch.

Finding Your "Ness"

Something else I noticed about the people I consider natural borns: Not only do they not overreach in their professional lives, but they are self-contained in their private lives as well. When we think of them, we tend to think in terms of the fortunes they're making, the hundreds of thousands of dollars, as though the money defines them and their success.

But for most of them—or at least those I know personally—it isn't a race to accumulate the most toys (well, for some it is). It's not that they're not competitive. It's just that they define success in other ways; usually this means happiness. I know this is beginning to sound like psychobabble, something I want desperately to avoid. But remember Robert from the last chapter, who went through years and jobs before he became successful? He put himself in a situation professionally where he could succeed.

Defining Success

The same thing holds true personally. The natural borns I know are content in all aspects of their lives, and that's what creates that aura of success. This is not a chicken-or-egg question: It's not success that comes first followed by happiness; it's happiness that drives success.

How do you define success? I can't answer that for *you*; everyone's definition is different. For me, the answer is being happy at work. I know that sounds trite, but for me it just happens to be true. Personally, I think the advice everyone is given by that odd uncle they meet at the wedding really is true: "Find your passion and you'll be happy."

For some people it might be a happy family life. For others it's health. For many, it's finding a proper balance between all these competing elements. I recently watched a movie on cable that was literally so bad I won't tell you its name so you don't think less of me for sitting through it. One of the characters urged another to find his "ness." By that he meant the character should find out who he is and what is at his center, and use that "ness" to build a life on that.

How does all this affect your ability to sell?

For one thing, when you find that "ness," you may conclude that you don't need as much money as you thought to find happi"ness." Just removing that pressure, the *need* to succeed, can change your attitude and improve your performance at work.

Frankly, though, finding your "ness" is easier said than done. People spend thousands of dollars on therapy looking for their "ness." It's not easy, but it doesn't mean you shouldn't strive toward that goal. The closer you get to discovering your "ness," the closer you'll be to acquiring a natural-born salesperson's positive attitude.

There are some smaller steps you can take along the way.

- Tomorrow always comes. Don't dwell on shouldabeens. You missed out on a sale you thought you had locked up, move on. Something good is due to happen soon.

- Try to have fun. You're not performing heart surgery; I don't remember ever seeing or even hearing about a sale that was a life-or-death matter. I used to put my cell number on my voice mail message: "If you urgently need to reach me, my cell number is. . . ." Then one day I asked myself, how much of an emergency can there be in sales training? Get some perspective.

- It's okay to stop and smell the roses (or the coffee). You're running from town to town or from appointment to appointment, stop and take a breath. If it's a beautiful day, stop at a park and enjoy the view. If it's the middle of winter, stop at a coffee shop, have a warm beverage.

- Look—in the real world, there are people who find the great job and are surrounded by supportive people. You may be stuck in a position you are not passionate about, but that doesn't mean you can't find something you can be passionate about. It doesn't have to be work-related. In fact, it may be better if it isn't. Perhaps there's a hobby that captures your fantasy. Or a volunteer opportunity. I know someone who tempers the obligations of his job by being a volunteer emergency medical technician with the volunteer ambulance corps in his community. He says it gives him a sense of accomplishment and keeps him going when he's at work on a boring project.

- Set some achievable goals in your personal life. Anne—that's my wife—and I sit down in December of every year to write down things we'd like to do over the next twelve months. It could be something as simple as a special vacation or a cooking class we want to take. The point is that it's something we both want to do, something we both look forward to, and something that creates positive energy in our lives.

WHAT TO TAKE FROM THIS CHAPTER

1. The person who accumulates the most toys doesn't necessarily win. My experience is that people who define happiness in terms of toys—expensive cars, McMansions—are generally not happy even after they accumulate every conceivable status symbol known to human kind.

2. Remember who you were when you first started. Your goals then were simpler: perhaps a house in the suburbs with a white picket fence or an apartment in the city. It's okay to want more as you become successful, but it's not okay to want so much that you lose sight of your "ness"—the person you were who made you successful.

3. When you focus mainly on acquiring more goodies for yourself, it becomes more difficult to concentrate on your customers' needs.

4. Find balance in your life. It can't be all work all the time. You will burn out, and that isn't good for you personally or professionally.

Chapter 7

Getting Back to Basics

Selling is not something the natural-born salesperson thinks about. It's just there. The best analogy I can come up with for you is to compare it to the way Ted Williams hit a baseball. They say that Williams was able to actually see the seams of baseballs as they were pitched to him.

This wasn't a skill that he'd practiced over and over again until he perfected it; it was the luck of the genetic draw: his vision and eye-hand coordination were such that in those fractional seconds from the time a pitcher released the ball until it reached the plate, Williams could decipher the kind of pitch it was and react.

What does this have to do with sales? Frankly, there are a lot of things we can learn from the Splendid Splinter, as he was known.

Let's discuss the significance of natural-born skills. There is a tendency to be resentful of anyone who has them. On the surface, it seems that everything goes their way. They make the big sales. They make the big bucks. They have a positive personality everyone loves. But a key phrase in this paragraph is "on the surface." Consider Ted Williams.

Interestingly, Williams failed in his attempts to manage teams in part because of his natural gifts. Everything came easily to him; he didn't have to think about it. As a result, he never examined how he did what he did, didn't understand it, and couldn't explain the process to ball players less gifted than he was. Williams was extremely frustrated trying to coach athletes who couldn't be taught something that came so easily to him.

Moreover, being jealous of a natural born is just a waste of energy. That he or she has a certain gift you don't have is not your fault. You didn't do anything wrong. In fact, if you want to blame anyone, blame your parents for not providing natural-born genes. But do not waste time on negative energy.

Remember, too, that Williams not only failed as a manger, he regularly failed as a hitter. In his best year, Williams only managed to get a hit four out of every ten times he had an official at bat. That means the man considered the purest hitter in the history of baseball failed 60 percent of the time.

I think that's an incredible statistic. The man who was the best ever in his line of work screwed up far more than he succeeded. That has to serve as a reminder of how important it is for the rest of us, the mere mortals, to keep things in perspective. Missing out on a sale is not the end of the world.

Another important point is that while Williams was naturally gifted, not all his colleagues were. There were and are a lot of people in the game who are not as genetically blessed as Williams was. Yet they managed substantial and lucrative big-league careers nevertheless. What they had to do was think about the things Williams never thought about. They had to break down what they did to its various components, figure out their own strengths, and work on their weaknesses.

It is exactly the same thing in sales. In the first part of this book I discussed attitudinal aspects of the sales process. Going back to a sports analogy, I'm sure Ted Williams was convinced he'd get a hit every time he walked up to the plate. And Michael Jordan knew he would score every time he drove to the basket. And Tom Brady believes he will hit his receiver every time he drifts back into the pocket.

That's important, because (as I've said, what, a dozen times?) a positive attitude is a major contributor to success—in any field, quite frankly.

Negative vibes turn people off; good vibrations (to quote the Beach Boys) work the opposite way.

The reality is that you can have the best attitude in the world, but that's not enough. Attitudes don't sell. You still have to come up to the plate and take a few swings. And that's the part we're going to pay attention to in the next section of this book. Like a coach, I'm going to break down and discuss various aspects of your swing. You probably won't need to work on everything. But you will have to figure out the weak parts of your game and concentrate on fixing them.

That's going to take substantial discipline. People are naturally inclined to do what they do well. But just that you're reading this book gives me hope that you're willing to do what it takes to improve your game.

What do I mean by concentrate? A natural-born salesman makes cold calls almost without thinking. He or she has the gift of gab and can convince a secretary to put him through to her boss.

Once connected to the boss, our natural born seems to know just how to convince her to set up an appointment. It's not easy, except to a natural born. What do the rest of us do? Practice these skills until they become second nature. We may never become .400 hitters, but we'll be able to make quite a nice living and reap oodles of satisfaction batting .300.

Breaking Down the Sales Process

Before we do that, let's examine the sales process. And it is a process. One step leads to the next in the way (to finally use a nonsports analogy) one word leads to the next in poetry.

There is a widespread belief in sales that it's important for salespeople to keep their eyes focused on the goal: a contract, an order, a sale. But that isn't or at least shouldn't be the goal. Your goal should be to get to the next step. Focusing on a goal that, depending upon your sales cycle, may be several months down the road, causes you to lose focus on the here and now.

Over the next dozen or so chapters, I'm going to talk about the various steps in the sales process: How to get them right every time; how to practice them so that they become second nature to you; how to become a better salesperson.

In short: How to get the natural-born salesperson jealous of you.

WHAT TO TAKE FROM THIS CHAPTER

1. Some people are born with a gift to sell the way Ted Williams was born with the gift to hit a baseball. Being jealous of them not only fills you with negativity, but it's also a waste of time and energy. It won't help you sell better.

2. More important, remember that in his best year, when he hit .400, Williams failed six out of every ten times he was at the plate.

3. Selling is a process with several steps. And it can be easy to improve—one step at a time.

Chapter 8

Climb Every Mountain

A couple of years ago, I read *No Shortcuts to the Top: Climbing the World's Fourteen Highest Peaks*, a memoir by Ed Viesturs. I'd never heard of Viesturs before I saw a copy of the book at my local book shop. I was attracted to it by the cover photo of the author in an orange jumpsuit kind of outfit standing atop a snow-covered peak.

Viesturs is a famous mountain climber, the first American to climb the fourteen highest mountains in the world—without using oxygen bottles. This of course raised an immediate question in my mind: Why? What possible reason would anyone of sound mind and body do that?

Intrigued, I purchased *No Shortcuts*, and was immediately taken in by what I discovered was his approach to mountain climbing. I have been quoting from the book ever since; Viesturs does something I've always done, but never really figured out how to anecdotally illustrate. Until now.

He plans every ascent backwards. That is, he starts off assuming he will get to the peak, and so he begins his planning process there. He doesn't plan when he's going to get to the top; he worries about when he has to leave the summit to get back to his last base camp while it's still daylight out.

Then—and only then—does he decide when he's going to start for the top. For the sake of argument, say that to get back safely to his camp while there's still light out, he has to leave a peak no later than 2 P.M. So let's say it takes eight hours to get to the peak and allow for an hour of rest, he can't leave base camp too late. That means he has to start out *no later* than seven in the morning.

Keep in mind that Viesturs' goal isn't to reach the peak. He starts out each climb assuming he will. His goal is to get down! If the weather—or the forecast—is bad when he intends to set out, he'll cancel the climb for that day. And, if necessary, the next day, too. And the day after that, as well.

Working Backwards Toward a Sale

What struck me as I read this is how much sense it made—and how closely it resembled the way I learned to sell. At the beginning of my career, I was like most salespeople. That is, I had one goal in mind: Close the deal as quickly as possible and move on.

The problem, of course, is that it almost never works out that way. Focused on the end of the journey, you may miss crevices and trip on your way there. However, working backward makes it easier to focus on the process and not the goal.

It took a while, but over the years I came to recognize that selling is a lot like a battle, and it doesn't make any sense to go to war until you understand what constitutes a win.

Like Viesturs, good salespeople start at the end, by deciding what it is they want to accomplish. Usually, it's to sign up a new client, get the contract, and make a deal, but that isn't always the case. Sometimes the idea is just to keep a client from switching to another supplier. But it isn't until you know the goal that you can begin to figure out how you will achieve it.

Let's say you are the sales rep for a paperboard manufacturer and through contacts in the industry you learn that General Mills is coming out with a new Captain Cheers cereal a year down the road. You want to supply the boxes for the launch.

You know your typical sell cycle is three to five months from the time of your first cold call until you get a contract. You are also aware that gearing up for manufacturing can take another two months. So you know you better get cracking right away.

Now that you've established your goal and begun working backward, you plan the steps you'll need to reach that goal—always keeping that goal at the forefront of your mind. Wrong! What you need to focus on is getting to the next step in the sales process. Again, if your focus remains on the end of your journey (or battle or climb or whatever metaphor you prefer) you may miss something in the here and now.

Moreover, a single-minded focus on a goal weeks or even months away bespeaks a lack of flexibility. One of the most important attributes natural-born salespeople seem to have is the ability to roll with the punches. It's not that nothing fazes them. It's more that they anticipate roadblocks and detours on the road; they just follow the "detour" signs until they can get back on the main road.

If you run into a roadblock when you're already thinking too far ahead, a diversion—even a simple diversion—can be discouraging and throw your entire effort off kilter.

Another point: I'm not immune to counting my chickens well before they hatched. It's a fault I assume I share with many of you. There have been times when I became certain I had clinched a sale too early in the process. I'd met with a prospect on a cold call and he was so enthusiastic about sales training and the need for it at his company, he did everything but sign a contract at our first meeting. I was fired up and had visions of sugar plums dancing in my head. Well, not so much sugar plums as hula dancers serenading me with their hips as I lay on a secluded beach on an outer island. (I'd actually thought this through and rejected Waikiki.)

I was daydreaming instead of concentrating on the process, instead of gathering information through the Power of Twelve, instead of considering how and what I was going to present.

You don't have to be a rocket scientist to see where I'm going with this story. I did not make the sale. There were numerous political and some practical situations I was unaware of because I did not do my homework. Had I planned backward, timing everything out, I don't believe this would have happened.

Patience Is a Virtue

Viesturs made two more points that I think are appropriate to us as salespeople. As noted earlier in this chapter, if conditions aren't right, the climber might stay in the base camp just below the peak of the mountain for days. Conditions aren't always right for salespeople, either. You can't rush success. If something is askew, there's no point in rushing ahead. You're much better off—and more likely to succeed—if you stop and try to figure out what's going on.

It may mean that things are unsettled at your perspective client and making a formal presentation now dooms you to failure. Or it may be that you're incorrectly interpreting the information you have. You may just instinctively know that something's wrong, but not be aware of what it is. Whatever the case, stop, do not pass go, and wait until you can figure out what is wrong. On a road trip, you don't go down the wrong highway just because you want to keep driving.

Small Steps—Or Don't Sweat the Small Stuff

In his book, Viesturs describes how physically draining mountain climbing can be. Because you're at the whim of the elements, it is a most capricious sport. So what he doesn't do is waste energy worrying about something over which he has no control.

Sometimes he becomes so physically drained, it's hard not to get discouraged. So he doesn't focus on what might be insurmountable—like getting to the top. Instead he creates a series of incremental goals; he breaks things down to manageable units: Get to the rock 100 meters away; make it to the snow drift up the hill.

There are valuable lessons in this approach. You can't always get the whole enchilada. Sometimes you're better off taking just smaller bites.

Again, Viesturs' book is called *No Shortcuts to the Top*, but from my perspective it might just as easily have been called *No Shortcuts to the Sale*.

WHAT TO TAKE FROM THIS CHAPTER

1. Planning a sale is like planning a war. You can't do it well until you know what your goal is. Once you establish your goal, it's easy for an experienced general (or sales rep) to plan backward and decide the steps that will ensure your victory.

2. Don't focus on the goal. Focus on the next step in the sales process. If your mind is on the future, you may miss important clues in the here and now.

3. You know what they say about the best laid plans of mice and men. Be flexible. You can't be so focused on a plan—even the right one—that you can't make adjustments. You need to be able to go with the flow.

4. Don't count your chickens before they hatch. Planning how you will spend the large commission check you're going to get is a diversion from your mission. I'll say this again: You need to get focused on reaching the next step in the sales process.

5. Patience is a virtue. Conditions are not always ideal for mountain climbing or sales. Wait until they are. Rushing blindly ahead in a snowstorm doesn't make sense.

6. There are times when it makes sense to take baby steps. You pitch a big account but are offered only a small piece of the business. That's not something you should be disappointed by; it's an opening for more. (See #5.)

Chapter

Getting Down to the Nitty-Gritty

In the preceding chapters, we spoke about what I think we'd all consider the ephemeral qualities possessed by natural-born salespeople. That is, they have a can-do attitude, are extremely verbal, and seem to react almost always correctly to any situation. These are in fact the characteristics that define the natural born.

But they are soft skills. The importance of a positive attitude and the kind of strong verbal skills that can help lead to a relationship can't be underestimated. But it's not the soft skills that close sales.

Let me repeat that, because this is important:

Soft skills enhance a salesperson's ability; they do not and cannot replace it.

It's the hard skills: sitting down at the phone every day cold calling leads, spending the time necessary to be certain you know everything there is to know about your product or service, preparing for meetings, making presentations that kill. That's what sells.

And in a perverse way, people like you and I who are not naturally gifted actually can get a leg up on those sons of a gun for whom everything comes so easily. What do I mean?

The example I use all the time is penmanship. Do you remember when you first learned cursive writing? Every letter had to be slanted perfectly; it was almost as if the characters had to be drawn on the paper, not written, with every tiny curlicue in its proper place. But as we got older, we paid less attention to the rules. I don't know about you, but I've gotten to the point where I can't even read my handwriting.

In my experience, it's kind of the same thing with natural-born salespeople. Many of those that I know are so used to success that they take it and the sales process for granted. It comes so naturally and easily to them that they glide through it without giving the process much thought. And that can be dangerous.

Recently, for example, a client asked me to talk to one of his salesmen. For three of the last four years, this guy had been the top salesman in the company. But over the last year his ranking had slipped. What his manager was concerned about was not that his sales volume was down, but that he had lost his touch.

"Jim [not his real name] was the best salesman I've ever seen," the manager told me. "He was a gosh darn [not the real words he used] natural. But there have been a few times over the last year when he came back and all but swore to me that he had just landed a major new account. And each time, the business went to [a competitor]. He's never been off his game like that."

I hate doing one-on-one critiques. It's too personal. Telling someone what they did wrong is not a good way to win friends and influence people. But the sales manager was a good client of mine, and saying no to him was not a good way to win contracts and influence clients.

To make a long story short, I met Jim. He was smart, understood why we were meeting, was extremely self-deprecating, and, as near as I could tell, was a very warm, nice guy. I could understand why his customers liked him. I liked him and enjoyed his company. (In fact, we still see each other socially.)

We set aside an entire day during which I went over four recent case histories with him—all sales he was convinced he'd made only to see the contract go to someone else. I reviewed his notes and call reports with him and took him through each of the sales from the initial cold call to the final presentation.

Frankly, the results were not surprising—at least to me. In each case, Jim relied too much on his soft skills. That is, he'd built up (in his mind) so strong a relationship with his first contact at a potential client firm that he sloughed off some of his responsibilities to the companies. And by companies I mean both the one that he represented and those that he was selling to.

In short, getting back to my penmanship analogy, he didn't dot his Is and cross his Ts.

Why did Jim risk transactions of that size by not doing all the prep work? Don't you think he'd automatically do all his homework, since three of these four cases were multimillion dollar deals? Obviously, Jim didn't make the mistakes consciously. He didn't say to himself: You got the deal, so do the bare minimum. But in these cases, the mindset of the natural-born salesperson actually worked against him. He knew he'd gotten his contacts on his side just on the basis of his personality and charisma. In fact, one of the prospects virtually promised him the business: "If I could, I'd sign the contract right now."

But perhaps because of that ingrained positive attitude that he and the rest of the naturals have, Jim missed the words "if I could." He heard them; they just didn't register. What he heard was that this was a done deal. So without thinking, he moved on from there to presentation. He skipped several parts of the sales process—including finding out what his client company really needed from him—and prepared a presentation.

The presentation—and he ran through it for me, slides and all—was okay, but it was less than it could, should, and would have been had he done all his homework. I think Jim knew he was in trouble before he set up his PowerPoint. When he first entered the conference room where he was scheduled to present, he was greeted by eight executives he'd never met. He had no idea what they did or why they were there. But soon after he started, it became clear that they were not as enamored of Jim's winning personality as his contact had been.

About ten minutes in, he was interrupted by someone who asked a question. It was a good—and very basic—query about delivery schedules to the company's three plants around the country. All Jim could say was, "I'll look into it."

Stuff happens, but they normally didn't happen to Jim—and certainly not four times in an eight-month period. From natural born he became a salesman who began to question himself and lack confidence. Although (and I pat myself on the back here) when I showed him where he went wrong, he bounced back pretty quickly.

What does all this mean for you? I believe lacking natural skills can work to your advantage. And to explain I must use a sports analogy. I've gone to numerous golf camps, where I've received intense instruction for several days running. By the end of the camp, I've played several rounds at four strokes below my normal average. (I should point out that that is not a sizable percentage gain, but still very pleasing.)

But then I get home, and within a month it's as though I'd never had a lesson. So I attempted something different this summer. I took a couple of lessons with my club pro and I asked him why I couldn't retain the lessons I learned at camp. His response was so obvious I was embarrassed that I'd even asked the question. He told me I just didn't try. When I had an instructor there standing by me, telling me how to distribute my weight, how to grip the club, and how far I should go back on my back swing, I did well. Okay. In the name of honesty I must confess that I didn't do well, but I did do better.

So, the pro said, clearly I was physically capable of improving my game, all I needed was to have an instructor with me all the time.

We both laughed and I said of course that's not possible. What, I wondered, was Plan B?

Be your own instructor, he said. Golf is a unique game in that it doesn't require split-second decisions. You don't have to return a serve coming at you at 130 miles an hour or decide whether to swing at a baseball coming at you at 90 miles per hour or faster.

"So make a list of all the tips instructors have given you and look at them as you approach every tee. Go over them in your mind as you address the ball. Be sure you dot every I and cross every T."

Of course, when he made the penmanship reference, it all became clear to me. If you're not a natural-born anything and want to improve, you have to work that much harder to be sure you do everything by the book. You can't afford to skip any steps the way a natural born might. You have to stop and examine every component of the sales process. Make a list of how you complete each part correctly, remind yourself of the rules, and then step up to the tee.

Or you can read the next few chapters where I've done it all for you.

WHAT TO TAKE FROM THIS CHAPTER

1. It's nice to have the gift of gab and a really good attitude. But the chances are pretty good that no one signed a contract with you because they liked the way you spoke or your outlook on life.

2. The bottom line of the bottom line is that no matter what ephemeral gifts you bring to the table, you also have to bring a proposal that makes sense.

3. Yes, working the process is something that usually comes naturally to the natural-born sales reps, but that doesn't mean you can't master those skills. It just means you have to work a little harder—dot every I and cross every T. Concentrate on the basics that the natural borns sometimes overlook.

Chapter  10

Warming Up to Cold Calling

No one likes to make cold calls. No one.

It's just natural for people to gravitate toward things that are fun and that they're good at. Prospecting isn't fun and I don't know anyone who is great at it. Cold calling is set up for failure.

You are largely calling people you usually don't know and interrupting them to ask that they do something they don't want to. Your greatest enemy as a salesperson isn't your competition; it's lethargy. If the person you call had a problem that required your product or service, he'd be calling you. So the assumption is that everything is going relatively smoothly at his or her operation. No one is yelling for change. So if he or she sees you, he risks upsetting the apple cart. If you make a strong case, he or she will have to go to their bosses and say, "Look, I want to do things differently. I've been doing something wrong. Instead of supplier A, I want to use supplier B."

Obviously, it's just easier for a prospect to say he's too busy to see you or he's happy with the status quo or he's on his way to Tahiti for an extended vacation.

I consider myself above average at making cold calls. It is not something that comes easily to me. My ratio of converting cold calls varies from about one in fifteen to about one in twenty. And those numbers are slightly inflated, because not all of my cold calls are cold. Some, as you'll see below, are lukewarm. But I've developed a system that increases my odds of success—and almost literally forces me to sit down at my telephone when I come in.

The System

The last thing I do before I leave my office every evening is create a list of at least fifteen companies I intend to call the next day. The list includes the firm's phone number (obviously), the name of the person I want to speak to (if I have it), the reason I'm calling this particular company, and the pitch I'm going to use.

Even if I've had a long and horrific day at the office, even if it means I'm late for dinner risking the Wrath of Anne (which is much worse than the Wrath of Khan; I'm not married to Khan), I sit down and prepare this list. I do it because I know that if I don't make the effort today, I'll find an excuse not to make the effort tomorrow.

My approach to cold calling is (to my mind, anyway) very logical. I try to start with the most obvious prospects, people I've worked with before. Clients change jobs, both within companies and to other companies. I always attempt to stay in touch with them—at least those who were happy with my work. But I also read newspaper business sections and numerous trade journals. I attend all kinds of conferences. I belong to fraternal organizations. I keep my ear close to the ground.

If someone I know or have dealt with in the past changes his or her job, I give them a call. I don't do this right away, of course. I give them a chance to settle in. And I don't care what their new job is. They may not be in a position to hire my firm, but they are in a position to recommend me to the person who is.

Priority number two is companies we've done business with before. I'm in a situation where I can come in and conduct a training program for a company's entire sales force. I monitor the success of the program, always, if only to see if any other course I offer is appropriate. But at some point I've done all the training I can do and have to say good-bye. Actually, I never say good-bye—I only say au revoir.

Because I always leave a note on a calendar to remind me when a company like this has to be re-contacted; usually I do it three years after I completed my last program there.

Number three on the priority list is companies similar to the ones I've already worked at. Obviously, I've developed expertise in that particular industry, I have a track record, and I can hit the ground running.

It isn't until I hit priority four that I make calls for which there is no logical explanation except that I am hungry and likely to be hungry tomorrow and the day after that as well. Even here there is some logic in the way I approach the task. I start with larger companies that are more likely than smaller ones to have corporate training programs. Because (as noted) I belong to a number of industry trade groups, I make it a habit to scour association directory membership lists. Therefore, my first set of calls goes to companies where I have a specific body I can ask for: "Can you connect me to Mr. Smith in your training department" or "I'd like to speak to Ms. Jones in human resources."

Guess what's down at the bottom of my call list. Right: Those calls where I don't have a specific name in the company, and I have to ask for someone by job function. That's the worst, because there have been times the person I ultimately hoped to reach actually picked up the phone and I had to get into a conversation with someone whose name I did not know.

As you might expect, this last group makes up most of my call list—as it likely does for every salesperson. That's why the success rate for cold calling is so low and why most folks will create excuses to avoid making these calls.

- Today is Don't Pick Up the Phone Day.
- I spilled some coffee on the phone.
- I have a cut on my dialing finger.

I understand that. I know that there are some among you who have achieved a certain level of success and feel cold calling isn't necessary. Or that you only need to prospect within your existing client base.

Let me put it to you as simply as I can: *You are wrong!*

Companies go out of business, they merge, the guy who replaces your current contact may not like the way you dress. That's all she wrote. Meanwhile, you still see a steady stream of checks coming in, so you're not too worried.

Again: *You are wrong!*

Subtle enough for you?

Here's the deal. I know that over a two week cycle—that's 150 cold calls—I will get about ten first appointments and of those ten I will be able to get eight return visits. And of those eight return visits I'm likely to generate one sale. But it will be about eight to ten weeks from the time I made the first call that I start a training program at this new client and maybe five weeks after that that I get paid.

So you're talking about a period of about four months from the time you make that first call before you get remunerated. I know that if I don't prospect today, I'll still get a commission today. But that's for work I did four months ago. Four months from now, though, my purse will be empty.

So, like you, I hate cold calling; fortunately I have greed to keep me going.

WHAT TO TAKE FROM THIS CHAPTER

1. No one likes to cold call. It's difficult. It can be humiliating. And it opens you up to the possibility of one failure after another. But you have to do it.

2. You can't rely on your existing book. Your biggest ally at Company A may retire, switch jobs, or even get canned. His or her replacement may not have the same warm and cuddly feeling toward you that his predecessor had. Not only do people leave, but companies do, too—through mergers, buy-outs, and bankruptcies. So it is imperative that you have a constant stream of new business.

3. Develop a system that forces you to make X number of cold calls a day. I prepare the day before, and after doing all that scut work (gathering phone numbers and names) I feel compelled to sit down at the phone the next morning. You may devise a different system. Whatever works. But you must sit down and make cold calls. Every day.

4. Set priorities on your calls. You have the potential to land some customers more than others. Work the percentages and start with those.

5. Again, no matter how you get yourself to the phone, you must do it every day until it becomes an ingrained habit. It's like (for me, anyway) exercise. It's tough to get out of bed at 5 A.M. every day to go to the gym. But after a while, it becomes a part of your routine. But find excuses to sleep late a few days, and you'll quickly fall out of the habit.

Chapter

Creating a Hit List

Cold calling is one area where the natural borns, with their ability to converse easily about almost everything, seem to have an advantage. In theory, they get through to prospects better than the rest of us, charm people better than the rest of us, and get appointments more often than the rest of us. But the problem is that they don't enjoy cold calling any more than you or I do.

So if there is one area where we can out-do the natural borns, it is in determination. That and a willingness to outhustle everyone else on the planet makes the difference between being successful and being an also-ran in a best-case scenario, and between success and outright failure in the worst-case scenario. The desire to succeed goes a long way toward triumph, and if you avoid making calls it doesn't make the slightest bit of difference how well spoken you are.

As I have mentioned several times, I have particular expertise in this area, because I was not born with this gift. I'm an okay cold call conversationalist. Actually I'm being uncharacteristically modest. I'm actually much better than okay. Today. But when I was a younger man, I envied those people for whom lively conversation came so easily. It always seemed to me that they were always surrounded at parties by almost worshipful people who seemed to enjoy and laugh at every pearl of wisdom the natural born uttered.

So when I first started cold calling it was extremely daunting to me. Understand that while I wasn't as fluid a conversationalist as a natural born, I wasn't a social misfit either. I was certainly capable of making small talk at a party—after I'd been introduced to someone. But talking to a faceless stranger on the phone was very off-putting to me.

In the beginning, of course, I didn't have a network of former clients I could call. Every call I made was cold. No, every call I made was frigid. My solution to this problem was very simple. If I couldn't be spontaneous, I could rehearse. That's where the list I mentioned in the last chapter started. I'd come in and make notes about what I wanted to say.

I didn't write out a speech, because inevitably that's what it sounds like; I didn't want to come across like a telemarketer. I'd like to tell you this system proved an immediate success. I'd also like to tell you I won the Mega-Millions lottery and am now retired. Sadly, I can't do either of those things.

But what I can tell you is that I had the determination to succeed. And what I accomplished, I did by trial and error. I took copious notes. I kept those parts of my pitch that elicited a positive response and discarded those that didn't.

When someone gave me a negative response early on in my career, I would do what I call a Ralph Kramden "hamina-hamina-hamina" (from the classic TV show *The Honeymooners*, for those of you still wet behind the ears). In other words, I didn't really have a response. But I made note of the typical negative comments. They tended to fall into neat groups. And as I became more familiar with them and more familiar with my product line and more comfortable cold calling (note I didn't say comfortable; I said more comfortable) I began to fashion stock responses.

By now of course, X years later—and no, that's a not a mistake; I'm just not going to tell you how many years later it is—I have it pretty much locked down. So the following sections cover some of the things I do when cold calling and why I do them.

A Former Client Moves to a New Company

I try to stay in touch with pretty much everyone I've ever worked with or for. For example, I know Tim, who's worked at a legal services company for the last twenty years, from two jobs before this one. He was a student in one of my sales training classes X (see previous note about the X factor) years ago. We e-mailed each other periodically. If he had a question, I answered it as best I could and promptly. In his next job he was named sales manager at a much bigger company, and after five or six months in his new position he called me. Together we created a training program for his company. Now he's an executive and we've had an ongoing relationship at his present firm for almost two decades.

However, the reality is that it isn't always possible to stay in touch. You get busy. Someone leaves a company and seems to fall off the edge of the earth. A lot of stuff happens, so that it is not unusual to hear that someone you've worked with but lost touch with has a new job. Obviously, the temptation is to call right away, congratulate her, and politely ask for business. Please resist that temptation. I've learned that if you barge in like a bull in a china shop you rarely get the results you want.

First of all, wait at least two or three months after the person starts the new job. Give him or her an opportunity to get the lay of the land at the new company, figure out where all the bodies are buried. You really have nothing to lose by waiting.

If she is charged with immediately purchasing whatever it is you sell and if she's had good experiences working with you, she will in all likelihood contact you. And, if not, two or three months is an appropriate period of time to wait to remind her that you are still around.

By the way, I never start off by congratulating them on the new job. They know why I'm calling. I know why I'm calling. But, for some reason, that approach always struck me as being too mercenary. I'm saying "I know you have a new job," however, the subtext is "now that you have a new job, what's in it for me?"

Usually, I begin by asking, "What's new in the real world?" What that does is immediately cast them as the expert while I merely exist in academia. They can bring up whatever topic they want—whether it's their new job or their (possible) need for your services. The key here is that you have a conversation going and the chances are good that if there's a sales pitch to be made, she will make it. Or she may refer you somewhere else in the new company that needs your product or service.

A Company You've Worked With Previously

These cold calls can be particularly touchy and negative. The people you worked with years ago are gone. No one knows you. I've gotten through to a new person in charge at a former client who point-blank asked me why I didn't stay in touch. (I decided not to tell him that I tried periodically, but he never returned my call.)

What I try to do in these instances is to make it seem as though I'm performing a service for them. "The reason I'm calling now is to see if the systems we installed are still in place and working. What I'd like to do is come in and talk to you about the best way to do that." Or: "Have you done any sales training since I finished my program three years ago? No. Well, based on that, I think we should get together." Or "Yes, well, I'd like to come in and discuss how that program can interface with my methodology." My experience is that it works 75 percent of the time.

A Company in an Industry Where You Already Have Clients

This obviously is a no-brainer. "The reason I'm calling today is that we've done some work with the XYZ Company, and I'd like to tell you about the success we've had. I think we should get together."

A Freezing Cold Call

You have to figure out what works for you. Because I work in so many different industries, I always attempt to tailor my end of the conversation to my prospect's business. *I never make generic calls.* And once I get a conversation going, the ball is in my court to keep it going. I ask if he's ever heard of me or my company. I talk about my expertise and experience. I make sure to mention my books. And at some point I ask for a meeting. *I have to ask for a meeting.* He's not going to bring it up.

The truth is I don't care what his response is. If he agrees to a meeting, great. If not, well, I am prepared for every objection. Most salespeople hear "no," say thank you, and move on to the next call. Whatever answer I get I just turn around by listening and asking a question: Have you ever thought about doing it this way? Yes? Well, I think we should get together. No? Well, maybe we should get together to talk about it? As long as I can keep a conversation going, I have a shot.

When I Don't Get Through

One of my strategies is to try to start making calls early. More often than not, the caliber of person I try to reach is a go-getter who is likely to come in early—well before his secretary. I figure I have a shot at reaching him or her directly.

But obviously it doesn't always work. I used to hate voice mail. Those contraptions left me even more paranoid than normal. Did the machine break down? Did the prospect get the message? Ironically, as answering machines and voice mail became more dependable, I began to ask the same questions about secretaries. Now I'm sorry when an assistant picks up the line.

If I leave a voice message, not only does the prospect get the entire message, he gets it the way I delivered it, with my inflections and all. Now if a secretary offers to take a message, I tell her it's pretty long and ask to be switched to voice mail.

I don't try to butter up a secretary or leave a cute message. It doesn't work. Making him laugh won't make an assistant deliver a message with more enthusiasm. It will still read "Mr. Schufferman called. It was about catching a train to a sail." If I leave a voice message, at least he'll know it's Steve Schiffman calling about sales training.

The other thing I don't do is hang up if I don't get the person. That is I don't do it anymore. I understand why some salespeople do it. You don't want to leave a dozen messages because you feel you look foolish or needy. It also hurts your self esteem. And if you don't leave your name, of course the prospect can't call back.

I learned long ago that it just doesn't work that way. If someone wants to do business with you, he or she will call you back. If they don't return your call, calling them until you catch them by surprise won't help you. It's just a big waste of time. I'll call three times: the initial call, one week later, and then two weeks after that. No return call is his or her loss!

WHAT TO TAKE FROM THIS CHAPTER

1. You don't have to be a rocket scientist to create cold calling-priorities. It's simple logic.

2. Start with places where you have an obvious connection: you know someone at the company or you've done business there before. A little lower on the scale are companies in industries where you've done business before.

3. Develop patter that works for you. The idea is to get a conversation started. Once you do that, once you have the prospect involved, the potential to reach the next step is there.

Chapter 12

You Got the Appointment, Now What?

I recently attended a conference and was invited to make up a foursome at a local golf course. The golf outing was part of the conference program. None of us knew each other. We'd all met for the first time at the meeting. So I thought it wisest to issue a warning to my new friends. (For the record, this was a different golf outing than the one I mentioned in Chapter 4. I can't help it if I leave every golf course with a good anecdote.)

While I enjoy the game, golf is just that, a game, to me. I don't take it as seriously as many other people, and I didn't want to spoil the day for the three others—or at least those of them who play the game far more intently that I do. So I told my partners-to-be upfront that I was a hacker and that it would be their responsibility to help me find my often errant golf balls. They laughed. All agreed, and said they were all there just to have a good time.

Well it turned out that our group was made up of three hackers (including yours truly) and one guy who could have been giving lessons. He was a natural. Later at the nineteenth hole, he told us that he'd been on his college golf team and at one point even considered a career on the tour. But he soon realized that the distance between him and the top-levels of players on the circuit was too great to overcome, so he happily became a very good club-level player.

As we quenched our thirst, I asked him a question. He was the first of our foursome to get to the course and arranged to rent a golf cart for us. At the time I thought that was pretty presumptuous, although it turned out to be a wise decision. It was a very long course and I prob-ably—probably? absolutely—would have been exhausted three-quarters of the way through without the cart. Out of curiosity, I wondered, how did you know to rent the cart?

It turned out that since he knew he'd be playing this course before he came to the conference, he scoped it out on the web. He knew where each of the eighteen greens were, how far they were from the tees, and the best way to reach them. He even knew which clubs he could safely leave home. In his mind, he'd played the course before he ever boarded his plane to leave for the conference.

Not only that: He also showed up an hour before tee time and went out to the driving range to limber up.

Meanwhile, people like me just showed up intending to have a good time and play golf like we always do. The analogy isn't perfect, I know, but his words crystallized in my mind the difference between the natu-ral-born salesman's approach to a first appointment and that of most salespeople. Most of us just go in and play the first meeting game the way we always have: We talk about our company, try to close a sale, and, if unsuccessful (which is usually the case), move on.

The natural born realizes that every course is different. He researches it and prepares in advance. He knows how he's going to approach every green. But more to the point, he understands that the first meeting is not about selling; it's about gathering information, moving on to the next step in the sales process.

So first let's talk about objectives:

1. You want to lay the foundation for a relationship. How do you do that? Principally, you do it by starting a conversation. I'm not one of those people who believes that all a sales rep is supposed to do is listen; he or she has to participate in a conversation. That's how people relate to each other in business and in the "real world."

2. You want to elicit information, enough so that you can go back to your office and create a proposal that makes sense. At the minimum you want to gather as much information about the company as possible, especially who they currently buy your product or service from, how they sell their product or service, and who they sell it to. In your premeeting research, you probably have learned much of this information. But this initial get-together will enable you to fill in the gaps and dig much deeper.

3. You want to get permission to dig deeper in the company, speak to more people. By that I mean not only executives who make purchase decisions but also end users who are the folks who can provide you with the most useful information.

4. You want to create a reason to come back for another appointment.

Above all, *you do not want to try to make the sale at that first meeting*. You just don't know enough to make an intelligent proposal.

Like that golfer, it all starts with the research you do before you even get on the course.

I sell sales training to companies in a variety of industries. Clearly, it's incumbent upon me (and you if you're in the same position) to sit down and do significant research before I sit down with a prospect. What do I mean by significant research? I want to know specifically what a company does. And by company I mean each of its divisions—even if I'm calling on someone who represents only one of many within a conglomerate. You want to get a feeling for how a company is doing, where does it make money, where is it not doing so well. You want to learn who its competitors are and how they are doing.

If what you sell is industry-specific, you probably are already familiar with most of the players in the field. By that I mean, if you sell parts purchased by airplane manufacturers, you probably know who your potential client companies are. But that doesn't excuse you from research.

I can't put it any simpler than this: If God didn't want you to do research, He (or She) wouldn't have invented Google.

Business is fluid. What's true today won't be tomorrow. Going back to the airplane manufacturing scenario, one day the European Airbus consortium leads the pack and the next an engineering snafu propels Boeing back into the lead. One day, airlines are buying every small jet they can get their hands on to fly routes between smaller cities and the next day someone says the skies have become too crowded because of the smaller planes.

Remember, you do not have to know everything. You need to know enough to start a conversation. Research allows you to do things. The first is to ask intelligent questions. If you ask a prospect what it is he does, you come across negatively. It's as though you couldn't be bothered to even find out what the company does.

What you want to do is ask about how the company does what it does. People like talking about themselves and what they do. All you have to do is give them a chance.

WHAT TO TAKE FROM THIS CHAPTER

1. Preparation is the key to cold calling. It is important that you know the company you're calling. You need to know what they do, have an idea how they do it, and, most important, how your product or service fits in the company's scheme of things.

2. Don't assume you know everything. Because you know what happens when you assume. The business world is fluid today. Buying habits change almost as quickly as gasoline prices.

3. At every step of the way—starting here with the cold call—information is the key to success. Demonstrating knowledge about the company you're calling is one way to get a conversation going. And, as noted in the last chapter, once you get the prospect involved in a discussion, the possibility of getting to the next step in the process is greatly enhanced.

Chapter

The First Meeting

The first time a salesperson meets a prospect is awkward at best; it's more like a blind date than a business session. You've spoken on the phone, but never met in person. Neither of you really knows what to expect. In some ways, it is even more surreal than most blind dates.

The thing about going on a blind date (as opposed to an unwanted fixup) is that both parties want it to work. Based on the word of a close friend or relative or e-mail from an Internet dating service, they come to the date with optimism in their hearts. Even the worst pessimists in life (assuming there are degrees of pessimism) somewhere deep within their bosoms hold a small kernel of hope that this date will change their lives, that they've finally found their soul mates.

But at a post–cold call meeting, it's really only the salesperson who wants the meeting. In almost all of these cases, the prospect is content with what he's doing. He likes his current supplier. If he didn't, he would have called you. That's why I say (time and again) that you have to remember that you're not battling your competitors on a sales call, you're fighting the status quo, a comfort level that makes change seem like too much work.

What do you want to accomplish at this first meeting? As with each step in the sales process, your ultimate goal is to get to the next step and all your actions should be focused on how best to do that.

I've divided what you have to accomplish into three different stages. They are not distinct sections; in fact, they overlap. What I call phase two is something you should be doing throughout the meeting. I've divided it this way to make it easier for you to understand the things you have to concentrate on.

Phase One

This is the feel-each-other-out phase, where you attempt to establish some kind of rapport. It's small-talk time as you begin the process of deciding if you'd made a "love" connection. It seems simple enough. You do it regularly in your nonprofessional life. And if you've been in sales for even a few years, you've probably developed some sales patter to start and hopefully keep a conversation going.

But nothing is ever entirely simple. There are nuances that you need be aware of.

Obviously, you want to make a good first impression. If you're not dressed to the nines, you're at least dressed to the eights. You have a firm handshake and you're ready to start wooing.

But remember, your prospect is also trying to make an impression. Like you, she has a certain image she wants to convey. While she's agreed to see you, she may have reached that decision in a moment of weakness. Or she meant to see you when you set up the appointment, but there have been developments since then and she was too nice to cancel at the last minute. Ask yourself: Is she a good hostess? Does she welcome you? Does she respond to what you're saying? Is she paying attention? Or is she concentrating on papers on her desk and taking phone calls. Be aware of signs (and more on them later) because they should influence your approach on the call.

The best way to build rapport is to engage the prospect, to get her talking. And the best way to do that is by asking a question.

Typically a salesperson will look around the office for a clue on how best to begin a conversation: a photo of the prospect in tennis gear or with her children or grandchildren, or cute drawings up on a bulletin board. That's an okay, if pedestrian, way to get a dialogue going. However, I usually try to stay away from strictly personal questions and try to relate to the prospect in a business way.

Most typically, I'll go: "This is a great office. How did you get this job?"

Again, this has to do with more than the words I say. My tone is excited, as though I want this job. The implication is: How do you get here?

There are several reasons for that particular question and questions just like it. For one thing, people communicate in stories. It's an opening for the prospect to tell a story—and, as a bonus, tell a story about herself. People like—no they *love*—to talk about themselves—and most don't get a lot of opportunities to do so. Finally, if you keep the discussion at least partially work-centric, it's far easier to make the transition to specific product-oriented questions.

It is easy for me to go from how you got this office and job to how long have you been responsible for sales training than it would be if I asked about the prospect's kids or tennis game. "So you have a lousy serve, but how does that affect your ability to buy sales training?" Somehow, that just doesn't cut it.

Phase Two

The average experienced salesperson probably already does a version of Phase One. He will ask questions and walk away with some information. I believe the difference between him and the natural-born salesperson is that he doesn't understand that what the prospect says is only part of the story. That he's only walked away with a piece of the information available to him.

In addition to the words themselves, the salesperson must be attuned to how the prospect says them: the inflection in her voice, the expression on her face, her posture; her overall reaction, not just her words, is where the salesperson is likely to find the true answers to his questions.

People in sales training say nonverbal communication makes up as much as 35 percent to 40 percent of a conversation. I don't know how anyone can come up with a figure like that, but certainly I agree that it is a significant part of, and plays an important role in, any conversation.

The prospect won't necessarily say, "Enough small talk. Let's get to the reason you're really here." That's impolite and no one wants to be impolite. But she will signal by her posture that it's time to move on.

The prospect won't necessarily say that there have been quality (or delivery or price) problems with a specific product, but it may show up if there's a change in her tone or if she suddenly decides not to answer a particular question.

There's something else that comes into play here, what I call the extrasensory phase. At some point, you get a feeling for how the meeting is going. Go with it.

If the chemistry is right, you know it. Every funny line you say gets a laugh. The prospect pays rapt attention to what you say. So you continue as planned.

But the opposite happens, as well. I've been at first meetings where I figured out what they did with the Berlin Wall. They reconstructed it between me and my prospect, and there was no way I was going to get around, over, or through it. I tried every weapon in my arsenal. Finally, I just said:

"Look, this doesn't seem to be going well. Am I very far off base here? Did I make some stupid mistake?"

I'll usually get one of two responses. Either the prospect, perhaps feeling a little guilty at her lack of attention, will say, "No, no, everything is fine. Please continue." By the way, I am a person who never underestimates the value of guilt. Inevitably when I get that response, the prospect at least makes a show of participating during the rest of our conversation.

The other answer I get is, "You're right. The truth of the matter is we're very happy with the supplier we now have and we're not going to make a switch." It's not the best answer you want to hear—but it's not the worst, either. What you don't want is a wishy-washy response, "Well, what you've said is certainly something for us to consider." It's just enough to get your hopes up and keep you working even though the reality is the company really has no intention of signing on with you.

At least, "No, we're not interested" means you can move on, hopefully content that you gave it your best shot.

Phase Three

At some point you get a signal to move on. The prospect asks, "How can I help you," indicating enough small talk. Or she looks at her watch. In any event, it's time to get down to business.

It's easier for me to start by saying what you *don't* want to do. You don't want to ask an open-ended question like: "I want this meeting to be productive, so tell me a little about your business." If a person came into my office and started a sales pitch that way, I'd ask, "If you don't know the answer to that question, what are you doing here?"

Another one of my favorites is, "I'm sure you have issues or pains with your present supplier that you want to talk about." Again, if there were significant issues or pain, the prospect would have contacted you.

Going in, you have to understand what it is that you want to learn. You need to discover what the company has done in the past vis-à-vis your product or service, what it does currently, and what its future plans are. You need the information to figure out how your product can do that better or cheaper.

What you want is an opening that will allow you to segue into the questions you want to ask. I usually begin: "Mr. Jones, before we get going would it be helpful if I told you about my company?" I get a positive response I'd say 99 percent of the time. But it doesn't matter. If the prospect says she's already familiar with me and my company, I continue almost the same way I would have had I given her a corporate biography.

"I'm just curious, have you ever met with someone from my company before?" Or, "Have you ever bought from my company before?"

The idea is to ask questions that will lead you to more specific questions about who the company uses now and what its future plans are. Obviously, I have this pretty much down pat now, but I didn't always. So after every first meeting I'd make notes about the questions that worked and those that didn't. I'd write down the responses I received and the answers I gave—or should have given. It took a while, but I got a handle on the situation. And one of the first things I discovered is that I tended to talk too much. It's possible to have a conversation with an economy of words.

It's not that I shouldn't have been speaking, but on review (as the NFL refs say), I found my sentences tended to be wordy and too long and my questions repetitive. But I didn't realize that until I reviewed my notes.

When you've mined your prospect for all the information you think you're going to get, it's time to move on to the Power of Twelve.

WHAT TO TAKE FROM THIS CHAPTER

1. There is only one purpose of a cold call—and it isn't to make a sale. Your job is to convince prospects that it makes sense to continue the conversation. You want them to see that your relationship has potential, that they and their companies will benefit by not ignoring you, and that moving on to the next step is a good idea.

2. Your first goal is to create some kind of rapport with prospects. You don't want to be their friend, but you don't want to have an antagonistic or adversarial relationship, either. I've made sales to some of the most obnoxious people in the world and they probably thought the same thing about me. But obviously it's a lot easier if you get along.

3. One of the easiest ways to build rapport is to have prospects talk about themselves. Everyone likes to talk about themself. I write books so I can talk about myself.

4. It's important to listen to what prospects say. Not just the words, but the way they say them. There are often as many openings for you in what is not said than in what is said.

5. Don't overstay your welcome. Build rapport, get the information you need, and arrange to move on to the next step.

Chapter

The Power of Twelve
(Part I)

If **you** have finished your first appointment with your prospect and have not been given a definitive "no," you are well on your way to making a sale. It may not happen when you want it to happen. It may not be as big a number as you want. But unless you do something to screw it up, I would bet on you. Without even knowing you. (Just to be safe, it would be a small wager—not the entire farm.)

It's not a lock, understand, but if the right person—that is, a decision maker or an important decision influencer—has gone this far with you, he or she is probably on your team. What do I mean by that? I mean that your prospect is amenable to change. It does not mean he will change. But, remember, it's not your competition that you're fighting; the enemy is the status quo. And if your prospect has expressed a willingness to move on, to consider change, well, you've won at least half the battle.

So what's next? The average salesperson takes the information he's garnered from a prospect and creates a proposal. These rarely if ever work. The reason is simple. In sales, as in everything else, information is power. And if you've only spoken to one person, there is little likelihood that you have the big picture—or the power that comes with it.

In fact, my experience is that if you speak to only one person what you're likely to get is just a superficial overview. That person knows his job—say he's the purchasing agent—but may not know the specifics of how your product is used on the factory floor. A person may know how it's used on the factory floor but not be aware of some greater political issue.

Here's an example of what I mean. Recently, a salesman came to my office and tried to sell me software. He asked me how fast my computers are, and I couldn't answer him. I know what I need them to do. I press the appropriate buttons to get them to do that and that's pretty much the extent of my knowledge. I could tell him how I use my computer and what I want it (and, by extension, my software) to do. But to find out how it does what I want it to do the salesman had to go to someone else for that perspective.

I am not a Luddite. I use computers all the time. But I also drink coffee all the time. I don't know how it's grown. All I care about is how it tastes.

So you want to get as many points of view as you can, as many perspectives on the company you want to sell to as possible. It's why I coined the phrase "Power of Twelve." That is, ideally you want to meet as many as a dozen additional people in the company (besides your cold-call prospect)—and it doesn't necessarily matter where they stand in the corporate hierarchy. Most everyone will provide you with an additional viewpoint, additional tidbits of information as seen from their perspective.

The more people you talk to, the more you find out about the company. It's as simple as that. How did I come up with the Power of Twelve? The answer is simple: Experience. I've found that if you talk to more than twelve people, the answers become repetitive. If you meet fewer, your knowledge is incomplete.

Everything is proportional. If the company you're dealing with is small, maybe there aren't twelve people to talk to. If you're talking about a product or service where the dollar volume is not great (nor is the potential to increase dollar volume) you may not want to invest that much time. But I have found that if I work with a dozen people in a company from the street level on up, I will likely know more about the company than the CEO does. But gathering information is only part of why going to the Power of Twelve makes sense.

The Power of Twelve may help you unlock additional sales opportunities you were previously unaware of. I know it's happened to me. I met with the CEO of a large company, and he introduced me to a senior vice president of the company, who I subsequently also met with. I asked him if I could meet other people in his company, so I could get a better feel for what his firm was about. He agreed and helped me set up appointments.

Ultimately I ended up meeting with exactly a dozen people, but what was really fascinating about this as far as I was concerned is that I discovered a division of the company that no one had mentioned to me when I was meeting with the upper echelon executives. It was run profitably by a manager in a plant.

I met with him, and he pointed out a couple of areas of need where we might be able to help them increase growth and profitability. When I went back to the CEO and senior vice president, they said they hadn't really thought about it. The company was so big that even though this division contributed black ink to the bottom line, it was so small it wasn't really on the radar. But, yes, they decided, my idea had potential.

The point, of course, is that had I not pursued the Power of Twelve at various levels in the corporate hierarchy, I never would have been aware of this division or gotten what turned out to be a decent piece of business.

Finally, the Power of Twelve can help you build allies in your quest. People at all levels of business today are suspicious when a stranger comes in and asks them questions about what they do. When I do my Power of Twelve, salespeople I speak to are recalcitrant at first. I assume they think I'm a company spy out to find ways to eliminate their positions. But as soon as they understand why I ask the questions I do—that is, I want to see if I can create a program that will help them earn much more money—there is no end to their cooperation.

Depending upon your industry, you may or may not run into a modicum of resistance, but you should easily be able to convert the skeptical into the convinced. As I've noted, people like to talk about themselves. Give them the opportunity to discuss what they do, how they do it, and how long they've been doing it, and often without prompting they'll tell you what's right with the current product they use and—more important from your perspective—what's wrong with it. If they like what you have to say, they will support your efforts. An assembly-line worker's support in a multibillion-dollar corporation may not sound like a big deal, but you know what gossips we all are. He might say something to his supervisor who may say something to his manager and so on up the ladder. You've probably spoken to many of these people anyway, and hearing that others support your initiative can only help your cause.

Setting Up These Meetings

How do you set up the Power of Twelve? You've concluded your first meeting with the prospect. You need a reason to come back anyway. And clearly you don't want to come back with a proposal because you know that without the Power of Twelve it will be incomplete. So I say something like:

"I'm willing to come back and meet with a number of your people to get a better sense of your company. That way I can put together a proposal that will ring true."

The typical response is, "What does this cost."

I, of course, respond, "Nothing. It is the kind of service we provide."

It's possible that the guy will say no, because he's really not interested in what you are selling. The reality, though, is that if he really wasn't interested, he would have let you know somewhat earlier in the meeting. More likely he is merely leery of having an outsider come into his company asking questions—for any number of logical and persuasive reasons. The next move therefore is up to you. Do you draft a proposal based only on this one meeting? Or do you bail?

Frankly, I've said I can't work this way and walked out on more than one occasion. I once went to a company and sat down with two top executives who told me I had twenty minutes to ask questions. Based on that, they expected me to send them a written proposal and they would only contact me if I won. I was competing against six other firms, they said.

That they wouldn't give me sufficient time to gather the necessary information was entirely unprofessional. Even worse in my book is that they didn't have the courtesy to let me know the results.

They were shocked when I took my materials (including the business cards I'd given them) and left. Ironically, five years later, after the two goofballs were gone, I got the business my way, by properly gathering information and putting together an intelligent proposal.

WHAT TO TAKE FROM THIS CHAPTER

1. A recurring theme of this book, my other books, and all my courses is that information is the key to success. The more you learn about a company, the more targeted your proposal will be, the more likely you will be to register a sale.

2. The Power of Twelve is simply my way of saying that it is important to dig deep within a company to get as complete a picture as possible. Everyone sees the company from a different angle. Ideally, so will you, once you've completed the Power of Twelve.

The Power of Twelve
(Part II)

I trust I have convinced you that the Power of Twelve makes sense on many levels. The next step is to figure out who you want to talk to and what you want to ask them.

I know the "whos" in my business, and I'm happy and anxious to meet with anyone from a sales assistant on up. Presumably you know who you need to meet within your industry. Depending upon your product or service, the people you need to speak to may be anyone from a plant manager or a guy who recharges the air conditioning system on up.

The most common mistake that most salespeople make is their reluctance to deal with the "common" man—and by that I mean employees who aren't executives or on an executive track. They figure talking to some guy on an assembly line is not going to help them clinch a sale. Well, that is demonstrably wrong.

Let's say the company you're calling on uses a lubricant similar to the one you sell. Suppose the assembly line guy tells you that no one likes that product. Suppose he tells you why. Suppose your product has a response to that objection. Do you think that might help you? Enough said.

So, you've sat with your prospect and gotten his permission to talk to people in the company. If you know the people by name, that's fine. Otherwise just give him the titles of the folks you'd like to speak to. Three or four is enough to begin with, and you can branch out from there.

Although personal visits are ideal, you have to take what you can get, even if it's just a phone conversation or an e-mail exchange.

It's important to understand that the more complex the sale, the more you need the cooperation of the buying company. If you're selling a commodity—paper clips—you probably don't have to see a dozen people. But if your product is something unique rather than a commodity—an important software system or a key component of the manufacturing process—the Power of Twelve is vital, as is securing the cooperation of the people you speak to.

Seventy-five percent of the work we do is prior to making a proposal, and much of that time is spent—or at least should be—gathering information. Ninety percent of all sales fail because the information we gather is incorrect.

I cannot say this often enough. Information will drive your proposal—and the sale. And sometimes the information you are given is incorrect. It's not willful; but the truth is that (as we all know) in corporate America, there are times when the right hand doesn't know what the left hand is doing.

For example, we pitched a company that currently uses a different sales training company. I was undaunted, and did exactly what I've advised you to do: I went out and did research. I spoke to the sales manager and reps in the field. Most of the company's sales reps get leads by knocking on doors rather than using the telephone. Top management wanted to encourage them to use the phone more.

The salespeople resisted. What I found was that the salespeople were really aggressive in what they did. They'd come out of one door and go in the next. Based on that, I came to my prospect with an entirely different program than the one he sent me out to design. I suggested a program that will get them in the door either to see someone right then or set up a future appointment. I couldn't have come up with that—and likely would not have come up with a sale—but for the Power of Twelve.

Similarly, a company that franchised retail stores in the sign business called me in to develop a program that could help their franchisees. Sales, they told me, were primarily store driven. That is, the owners waited for people to come into the store.

Again, I followed the same rules I prescribe for you. I went out and talked to the company's top franchisees. And I discovered—surprise, surprise—that the bulk of their sales were not driven by random walk-ins. Instead, they actively went out and networked. They were visible in the community, and went out to see as many people as possible. Had I assumed that the corporate people were correct and not gone out and conducted a Power of Twelve, I would not have come up with an appropriate proposal that eventually led to a sale.

In preparing for these meetings it's important never to lose sight of why you are spending this valuable time asking questions when you could be out selling. Your main goal is to get answers to the four key questions that will go a long way toward helping you clinch the sale. Do you have the:

Right person? Through no fault of your own, you may have met with someone who is not the decision-maker and cannot even influence (or has minimal influence on) the final decision. It happens. One of the things you need to do is confirm who will ultimately say go or no-go when it comes to your product, and when you do that find a way to get him involved—either as part of the Power of Twelve (preferably) or at the presentation. The metaphysical question is if you make a great sales pitch but the right person doesn't hear it, have you still made a great sales pitch? The real-world answer is "no."

Right product? Obviously, you're not going to sell even the best automobile tires to a company that manufactures trucks. However, what you sell doesn't have to be an exact duplicate of what the company currently uses. If it is different, though, it really ought to be better in some way—easier to use, easier to maintain, and so on.

Right price? This is a no-brainer. You have to find out what your prospect is paying now. By that I mean the cost of the product or service, delivery charges, if any, and downtime because of quality issues. A high-volume copier doesn't do you any good if you get paper stuck every other time it's used.

Right timetable? You have to find out what the customer's buying cycle is to ensure that you can have product when he or she wants it and can get it where he or she needs it. And you have to be certain that you can continue to supply it in needed quantities.

I did a seminar recently for a company where we examined real-world pitches of a group of salespeople for a large corporation. Invariably, each proposal was missing at least one and often two of these fundamentals. Although there's probably not an exactly direct correlation, these missing elements reduced the salesperson's chances of success by 25 percent to 50 percent.

Again, the most important thing you can do is keep people talking, and one of the best ways to do that is ask about them—how they got the job, why they chose that career, how they do their job, how they think it might be done better. The idea isn't to come in as an inquisitor, but as someone who is curious and genuinely wants to understand what they do, how they do it, and how you can help.

It is important that you take notes, for a couple of reasons. The average guy will leave a meeting and make a minimal notation in whatever customer relations management software program he uses: "Saw Tom. He's interested. Call back." Clearly that's not enough information. In all likelihood, that entry will prove meaningless the next time you refer to it.

You need to have a record of what was said. If these sessions go well, a lot of different and important topics will come up. And it is imperative that you remember the conversation accurately so when you sit down to prepare for the verifying step (see Chapter 17) you will be able to accurately recreate your conversations.

But on a more subtle level, taking out pen and paper is a sign that you think this conversation is important, and that will encourage the person you are speaking with to go on at greater length and reveal more details. Nothing gets a person to speak more than the knowledge that the person he is speaking with is actually listening and finds what is being said important and fascinating enough to take notes.

In fact, when starting I typically ask for permission to take notes because "this is important and I want to get it right."

One caveat: You don't want to keep your face buried in your notebook or pad. You have to temper your note taking with observation, looking at the person you are speaking with—not just out of politeness but also for nonverbal signs that might reveal even more info than what he tells you.

There are certain things you should be looking for. Their absence doesn't mean you won't get the sale. But it will reduce your odds and make your job that much harder.

First: In the same way that you want to work for a company that offers you the right environment for selling, it's a lot easier to sell to a company that has the correct environment for buying. If it is an insurance company, you hope the company and its employees are focused on selling insurance and not on some internal political squabble. If it's a software company, the people should be focused on selling the software, and not on the latest takeover rumor and stock options.

Second: You have to be concerned about the competencies of the people you're dealing with. That seems like a strange thing to say, but if you're dealing with bureaucrats—people who have been doing their job one way and can't think outside the proverbial box—you're a goner. You must work with people who are bright enough to understand what you are trying to do and how your product or service can fit into their company. It sounds strange at first, but the people you deal with must be bright enough to get it.

Third: Finally the company has to have a culture that encourages competencies and sharp people doing sharp things and excited by the things they're doing. Google is like that now. But who knows how long that spirit of innovation will last? Eventually, all companies become staid, institutionalized, and tired. They've done the same thing for thirty years and it's really difficult to reinvent yourself. Look at GM, Ford, and Chrysler, which have pretty much conceded innovation to the Japanese auto companies. The American companies are tired; Toyota and Honda are not.

There are very few Googles in the world, and you are going to have to sell your products and/or services to the GMs and Fords. But it's important that you understand the signs and modify your approach based on the signals you receive.

In any case, though, you want to take the information you receive and get back to your contact within two weeks. The longer it takes before you and the prospect get together for a second meeting, the less likely you are to make the sale.

WHAT TO TAKE FROM THIS CHAPTER

1. Don't succumb to the temptation to deal only with executives. It's a common mistake. Sales reps often feel they ought to be dealing only with people in a position to effect a purchase decision. However, in the current corporate culture, operations have become so large and widespread that the left hand often doesn't know what the right hand is doing. Heck, sometimes the pinky doesn't know what the thumb is up to. Very often it's the people at the bottom of the corporate totem pole—for example, the folks who work on the assembly line—who can provide the information that can clinch a sale.

2. A basic rule of thumb is that the larger and (hence) more complicated a sale, the more people you should see to gather information for your proposal. But the Power of Twelve is more than just an exercise in collecting information. The more people you see, the more people you involve in your quest, the more allies you'll create. If a person gives you advice that you incorporate into your presentation, he or she is vested in it and will likely be a supporter of your cause.

3. Very often the Power of Twelve reveals additional needs you can fill.

4. Take notes. It's important you accurately record the information people offer. Also, it makes them feel that what they're saying is important and encourages them to continue.

5. Don't sit on the information. Get back to your initial contact with a preliminary proposal in two weeks or less, while this is fresh in everyone's mind.

Chapter  16

Figuring Out What It All Means

You've seen all the people you need to see and gathered all the information you can. Among the things you've learned is what the company has done in the past, what it is doing now, and how and why they are doing it that way.

Most important, you need to figure out what they are trying to accomplish. I stress again, you are not fighting your competition. You are fighting the status quo. You have successfully taken the battle to the enemy, and by getting this far you are close to victory. Your prospect has seen you. You've been allowed in the inner sanctum. Now you have to figure out why.

Why is the company willing to look at a different supplier? Is it looking for a cheaper price? Is it unhappy with the quality? Has the current supplier been making deliveries late? If you figure out what the company hopes to get out of its meetings with you, it will be much easier to get what you want out of your meetings with the company.

The natural-born salesperson probably got a sense of what he was looking for as he asked the questions. But for people like you and me—well, at least me—it takes longer. I actually use a study technique I learned in college several years ago. (I make a point of not being specific about how many "several" is. Suffice it to say I paid $35 for the course at a time when thirty-five bucks really meant something.)

The technique meant gathering in one place all the notes I'd taken on a particular subject—both from my textbooks and lectures. Slowly I'd begin the process of crossing out the material that I was sure was superfluous. After a while, I'd be left only with the vital material I needed to study and know. It made my student life much simpler because it forced me to focus on what was important.

That's what I do with my Power of Twelve notes. I spread them on a conference table and examine them one by one. I eliminate parts of the conversation that are peripheral to my mission. For example, while I took note of the fact that the sales manager and I were in the same college fraternity, that's not central to my current mission. So out it goes.

Before too long, a pattern begins to emerge. It may not always be clear-cut, but usually it is. Someone on an assembly line tells you about the difficulty of applying a competitor's product because bolt holes don't always line up properly. A plant manager complains because of inordinate down time because parts have to be replaced in inordinate numbers. Someone in customer service notes that the number of customer complaints related to this part has gone up for the last three months.

At some point, as I winnow down the comments to the essential, something jumps out at me. I recognize that this is the way I can help the prospect company. It didn't always happen that way, but I've been doing this for several years now (see previous note about "several"), so it's become easier.

I was lucky in the beginning in that, in my early years in sales, I had a couple of really good managers. And by good I mean that they were consistently positive and willingly worked with me to help me improve my skills. I learned early on that I can be too close to a project, and that a second set of eyes can provide a better perspective.

Depending upon the culture at your company, it can be helpful to ask colleagues for advice, to see if they've ever faced the kind of situation you are facing and how they handled it. Another good source is friends who work in other industries. They may be doing something in their business that is applicable in yours.

I made another discovery, this one by accident. There's a saying about "sleeping on it" before you make a decision. It works! I can't tell you why, but often when I've been wrestling with a problem, the answer comes to me in the middle of the night. By often, I don't mean every week—thank goodness I don't have that many problems anymore. But I'd say at least half the time when I go to sleep on a day when I've been searching for the answer to a particular problem, I wake up with something—the answer I've been searching for or a clue that leads me there.

Another helpful hint I can't stress enough is that you must know your product(s) inside and out. This is important for a couple of reasons. If a company is going to switch from an existing supplier to you, the people there will likely need the assurance that you are a professional. There are enough amateur salespeople around, and if they wanted an amateur effort they could just as easily stick with the company that's screwing up their orders now.

But as important, because you know your product so well—and now you also know the prospect's operation so well—you can make suggestions on additional uses for your product that no one at the prospect company had thought of before.

Remember, you are searching for those key elements that will help the executives at your prospect company get off their collective duffs and switch from another supplier to you. The first thing that comes to mind, of course, is price. But that usually isn't as great an issue as it appears to be. In a study we conducted, we found that price is not nearly as significant a factor in the minds of buyers as service. That said, service is more difficult to explain. As a result, most salespeople figure they're better off telling a prospect that they can save them $100 rather than say my company's service is exceptional.

However, if you can find a way to do that—demonstrate service, for example—it's as close to a guaranteed sales clincher as you can have. Assuming, that is, that your service is really good.

At presentations, a software company I know asks prospects to get the answer to a certain question from the customer service department of the company they currently use. The salesman also asks one of those present to call his company. Invariably the person calling the salesman's company gets a response while his colleagues are still on hold. His phone was answered by a live person—in America—and the "problem" was immediately resolved. No FAQs, no "all our customer service reps are busy," and no language barriers. How can you do better than that?

WHAT TO TAKE FROM THIS CHAPTER

1. Gathering information isn't the end of the Power of Twelve line. Once you have it, you need to interpret it.

2. Your competition isn't another company; it's lethargy. If no one is complaining, the tendency is to stand pat. Your job is to sift through the information you've gathered to find what prompted the company to consider a different supplier. Was it price? Delivery problems? Quality issues? Once you identify the problem, you're in a position to provide the solution.

3. It's always better to demonstrate a solution's impact than to just talk about it. Saying you are a penny-a-widget cheaper than the competition isn't nearly as effective as showing how, over the course of the year, the prospect can save hundreds of thousands of dollars.

Chapter

Verification Meeting

The most common mistake salespeople make at this stage is that they put together a proposal expecting to clinch the sale at a verification meeting. That's not to say it doesn't happen. It does, but rarely and usually only under certain circumstances. (More on that later.) The more likely scenario follows:

You've done your Power of Twelve and studied your findings. You've come up with an idea on how to differentiate yourself from the prospect's current supplier. You've found a way you, your company, and the product or service you sell is superior and you've returned to your prospect for a second meeting to sound him or her out.

Your goal now is to be "righted." I tell students that the opposite of wrong is right and the opposite of right is wrong. During this session, if you suggest something that's wrong, the prospect will undoubtedly correct you. This process accomplishes two important tasks.

First, it keeps you from making a silly mistake at a formal presentation. Just as important, when the prospect corrects you and puts you on the right path, he or she somehow becomes vested in you, an ally.

This should be the simplest part of the sales process. Thus far, in every step along the way, you've had at least the tacit approval of a company representative. You've been invited inside to see how it operates. Clearly, this indicates the company is ready for change. You have all the information. You've organized it. What can go wrong?

Plenty, actually. But first let's deal with what you can do to make everything go right.

To prepare for verification I write a proposal. Literally. I sit down and write it out, word for word, as though I was preparing for a speech (which, in effect, I am). I do this for a number of reasons. First of all, writing is the way I think best. Seeing an idea down on paper crystallizes it for me. That's pretty much the way I organize everything. You may be different, but if you never tried it I suggest you give it a shot. I think you may be surprised at how effective a tool it is. It forces you—or at least it forces me—to think critically.

When I'm finished, I synthesize it down to talking points that I keep in front of me on index cards. I usually do not need to refer to them—I've gone over the "speech" a number of times both in front of other people and in my head. But the fact that I have these notes in front of me shows that I've put some thought and effort into preparing for the meeting. (At this juncture, I don't usually do a PowerPoint. This is not a presentation. This is really just an informal get-together so you can better prepare for a presentation.)

What I do next is bounce my verification proposal off a couple of the people in my office who I trust to give me a sound, intelligent reading on my suggestions. This is really important and I can't stress it enough. In my office, I'm the boss, and I know that there are some people in my organization who will agree with everything I say. I don't want to bounce ideas off them. I want people who'll tell me a proposal stinks (if it does) and aren't worried about being politically correct.

You have to do exactly the same thing: Find people in your organization who are willing and able to provide you with an honest and intelligent critique of your ideas—and bounce your proposal off them. If it's your sales manager, so much the better. That's actually what he's paid to do. If it's coworkers, that's fine, too. The operative words there are honest *and* intelligent—both.

Once they're happy and you're happy, there's only one other person to please—and that's your prospect. At a meeting with him or her, I generally start off with something like this:

"I had an opportunity to meet with a number of your people. I think I've uncovered a couple of ways where I can help you and what I'd like to do is share some of those ideas with you." I will usually make a self-effacing comment such as "I think I'm pretty close," which I believe invites correction.

Typically I view a verification meeting as one with a four-part agenda: a report on *who* you've seen, *what* you've seen, a *conclusion*, and the *next step*.

From my opening, which suggests that I want to be "righted," I move on to a report of *who* I've seen. I tell the prospect that I've met with so-and-so and been to the plant and out in the field with three of the company's salespeople. This is important because, as with the index cards, I want the prospect to understand that what I'm about to suggest isn't something that I threw together off the top of my head. I put some effort into this and there is a very real possibility that I've put together something that makes sense.

Then I explain *what* I found out from the people I saw. That the people on the assembly line feel the current lubricant is too thick or too thin or too gray or too brown.

Then I tell them what I *concluded*—essentially that the company should buy from me because my lubricant is thick or thin or rich, vibrant colors. I can deliver it in whatever quantities he wants, where he wants it, and at a price comparable to the current supplier.

There are really only two things that can happen here. First, the prospect can agree with your analysis. In that case, the next step is relatively simple. You arrange for a time when you can make a formal presentation. If you're selling a small order to a small company where your prospect makes the purchasing decision, you may—and I stress may—be able to physically close the sale right there and then. But if there's any heft to what you're trying to sell, especially since you are unseating a long-time incumbent—you will likely have to come back with a formal presentation for the prospect and several of his colleagues.

There is, of course, another possible outcome. It could be that your prospect disagrees with you. For example, he might feel your analysis is incorrect. He may insist that the plant will never purchase red or white lubricant; at best it will go for mauve. Or the delivery schedule you suggested is too slow or too fast or somehow incomplete.

This isn't necessarily a bad thing. What should your response be? First, of course, you can agree with him. "Gee, I never thought of that," you say. "This puts everything is a new light. Look, I have to rework my numbers. Can I come back tomorrow at around 10:00 and show you what I came up with?"

But a prospect isn't always right. No one knows your product or service as well as you do. Through the Power of Twelve, you now have a good idea of how your prospect company operates. You have every right to fight for your beliefs. Well, fight might be overstating it, but you don't have to be a pushover either. You can counter by saying what about this or this? But generally if a person is correcting you, he is correcting you correctly. So go with it. Re-do the proposal with the corrections in mind, and immediately make an appointment to re-propose.

This all seems so simple and straightforward. What can possibly go wrong?

1. You can get too cocky. There are people who believe that because the prospect and his or her company have cooperated so far, they are committed to buying from you. That's not true. It's important that you pay as much attention to detail here as you do in any other part of the process.
2. You assume a negative posture. Again—and I can't stress this enough—the purpose of this meeting is to be sure everyone is on the same page. You have to word your proposal in such a way that it is clear you not only are receptive to being corrected, but you also welcome corrections.

3. You are completely off base. You might have completely misinterpreted what you heard in the Power of Twelve. You might not have been aware of political undertones. It can't be corrected.

4. You don't accept correction. I know salespeople who've gone to verification meetings so sure of themselves that they encourage being righted, but then refuse to modify their proposals with the new info. It just doesn't make sense.

And now, logically, you have to prepare a presentation.

WHAT TO TAKE FROM THIS CHAPTER

1. If you've gone this far, the chances are that you are well on your way to a signed contract. But the operative words in that sentence are "chances are." There are still a lot of potholes you can stumble over. The most obvious is that you have interpreted your Power of Twelve findings incorrectly.

2. Before you make a final presentation, give yourself an opportunity to be "righted"—that is, bounce your proposal off your prospect and get his or her reaction. If you're in agreement on major points, it's time for the next step. That next step depends on the size of the order. A small order and you may get a contract right then and there. If it is really a significant size, you'll likely have to make a formal presentation.

3. But what if your proposal is off base. No problem. Your prospect will likely correct you. And in doing so he vests himself in it. It will be difficult for him to argue against your proposal when he in fact helped draft it.

4. If valid, as they usually are, incorporate these suggestions into your proposal and ask for an immediate appointment so you can re-present.

Chapter  18

Prepresentation Planning

The art of presenting has changed significantly since I started selling. In that period, dinosaurs vanished from the face of the earth and using a felt tip pen and easel was no longer considered high tech.

Yes, I exaggerate. But the point is that the whole world seems to be moving faster now and as salespeople we have to keep up. If you do not, you clearly run the risk of becoming a dinosaur. We live in a youth-oriented society, and you are either with it or without.

In many ways, computers have made the sales job easier. Relationship management software allows you to track many more things than my father ever thought of during his sales career. It allows road warriors to keep up with the latest e-mail, inventory, and pricing from their hotel rooms and from their rental cars. PowerPoint allows us to make extremely sophisticated presentations unimagined a decade ago.

Question: Is this good for salespeople?
Answer: Of course it is.
Question: Is this bad for salespeople?
Answer: Of course it is.

One of the things I've noticed is that while presentations today are of high *technical* quality, they frequently lack *creative* spark. There are several reasons for this.

1. For many of us Luddites, the technology is so daunting we concentrate more on getting that right rather than on the content.
2. As computers have become more powerful, it has allowed software manufacturers to add bells and whistles to programs that make them easier to use—if you use the preformatted presentations. So that's what we do.

As a result, many salespeople prepare presentations to fit Power-Point rather than use PowerPoint to illuminate major themes of the presentation. And what inevitably happens is that salespeople—all of us—fall into the trap of using the same presentation time and again, the same slides in the same order, merely changing the customer's name and a few numbers. It becomes boring for us—and it becomes boring for our customers, who probably see the same slides at most presentations.

The theme of this chapter is that, as with everything computer related, what you get out largely depends on what you put in. If what you put in is geared to the machine and not the audience, what you get out will likely be a been-there, done-that kind of presentation.

There's much more on preparing the actual presentation in the next chapters. Here we concentrate on how we need to prepare ourselves for the presentation. For one thing, PowerPoint is not always appropriate. For example, if you are presenting just to one person or just a couple of people in an office, you are better off printing out your slides and using them to illustrate your (now non-power) points. In an office setting, you'll be working directly off your computer. Sometimes the screen is not easily visible from certain angles or if the lighting is off.

When you get to larger groups, PowerPoint is almost mandatory. Almost. There are no absolutes in sales. Absolutely. You have to meet your prospect's expectations. So if it's one man who works for a high-tech company and he wants PowerPoint you give him PowerPoint. If it is a group that seems to prefer a more personal approach, so be it.

Group size, however, isn't the only factor to be considered. The more complex your presentation, the more numbers and statistics involved, the greater the need for some form of visual aid—even if it's only a flip chart. It's important to note that no matter what kind of visual aid you use, people learn visually. Visual aids usually can't hurt and more often than not will help you make a point.

On the subject of group size, from your perspective you want the group to be as small as possible. The more people involved, the more difficult it is to reach a consensus. Without consensus, it's easy for even one negative person to get his or her way. After all, why switch? We already have a supplier. And the devil you know is easier to work with than the devil you don't.

A very large group also makes preparing a presentation more difficult, since some people will be familiar with you and your product and for others everything you say they'll be hearing for the first time. So who do you write your presentation for? Do you make it sophisticated, and lose the newcomers? Do you make it simple and lose the people who know and perhaps even support your petition? Or do you walk the middle ground and potentially lose everyone?

Of course, you have little control over the size of the group. But you can offer some input—especially if you've developed a decent relationship with your prospect. Suppose the group is larger than you'd like. What I've done many times is ask if that large number of people is typical for the company. Usually the prospect asks why, and I'll say my experience is that the presentation works better with smaller groups because (A) I use a lot of complicated statistics, (B) it's very sophisticated, or (C) whatever reason seems appropriate to make the point.

I've had a prospect reduce the number of attendees when I raised the issue. In fact, I remember one once told me that making the meeting smaller made sense, and that there were a lot of people who didn't really have to be there anyway. But, frankly, more often than not, the prospect said no change is possible, that's the way his company did things.

In either case, I always ask for the names of people, in part because I try to personalize the packets I leave behind. It's a little touch that I found is appreciated—and also is a great excuse to get me everyone's name. I generally recognize the names of many if not most of the people slated to attend the presentation; likely these are some of the same people I spoke to in the Power of Twelve. If I don't recognize a name I am invariably comfortable enough with my prospect to ask who the newcomers are and why they were chosen to be there. This enables me to separate the wheat from the chaff; my goal is to discover who the decision-makers are and which people are excess baggage.

If I have a better-than-good relationship with him or her, I might ask about the newcomers' agenda. I'll take my chances if everyone comes to the presentation open-minded. But if someone has ties to the existing supplier, it may help me to know that. There may not be anything I can do about it, but information is power. Who knows what angle I can come up with?

But even if I'm told everyone attending the presentation is on my side, I will seek permission to contact all the newcomers before the meeting—if only to bring them up to speed. This way, I tell the prospect, we won't have to waste the entire group's time bringing just part of the group up to date.

Then I call each of them, ask if I can send them material about the presentation, and conclude by saying something like: "By the way, has anyone filled you in on what we're doing? If not, I'd like to tell you about the program, because I think it's very exciting."

In theory, by the time you've reached this stage of the sales process you ought to be coasting. But that doesn't mean you can be sloppy.

WHAT TO TAKE FROM THIS CHAPTER

1. It's not the medium, it's the message. Don't let the bells and whistles of presentation software get in the way of making your point. Customers may be impressed with your mastery of technology, but they won't be swayed by it. Whether or not you make a deal depends upon your ability to find solutions for your prospect.

2. Group size is the primary factor in figuring out what kind of presentation you make. The larger the group, the more likely you'll wind up using PowerPoint.

3. To the extent that you have any control over numbers, the smaller the group to which you present the better off you are. Larger groups always seem to contain at least one naysayer, and naysaying is contagious.

4. Ask for the names of the people who will be attending. If asked why, say you like to personalize the leave-behinds. (By the way, that is a good idea in any event.) I then ask (and usually get) permission to contact the people whose names I don't recognize—that is, people I haven't spoken to as part of my Power of Twelve search. I try to get in touch with them all, to see if I can provide any assistance bringing them up to speed before the meeting.

Chapter

Preparing the Presentation

I've long felt—and many experts in the field agree with me—that writing and speaking are related. The more well spoken one is, the better one writes. Conversely, the better one writes, the more well spoken one is. Tied to that is my belief that the best writing is conversational in tone. You don't need to use big words to impress people.

So if my analysis is correct (and of course it is), the natural-born salesperson has a big leg up when it comes to preparing a presentation. She's got the gift of gab, so presumably that translates into a decided advantage when it comes to writing a presentation.

I wish I could tell you that that isn't true. It is. But the key to remember is that it is not an insurmountable advantage. Quite frankly, the physical act of writing the presentation is the easiest part of the sales process. You've done your homework. You've gone over your homework with your prospect. He's made corrections and/or approved your ideas. So really now it's simply a matter of dotting the Is and crossing the Ts.

Your job is to convince them that you have a decided advantage over anyone else who might offer a similar product or service. Typically, a presentation follows a particular pattern. It's relatively easy, therefore, to plug in your numbers, your delivery speed, your whatever. However, that doesn't relieve you from the responsibility of doing so creatively.

What I've noticed a lot of, though, is that salespeople prepare their presentations in PowerPoint—that is, they follow the preformatted default paths set by a programmer in Seattle. What I suggest you do first is write out the program separately from any presentation software.

First, make a list of the key points you want to stress. It may be your pricing structure, your customer service facilities, the quality of your products, your on-time delivery. Put them down on a piece of paper in order of importance. Remember, you don't want to stress only those points that are important to you; you want to push the points that are important to your potential client.

For example, let's say you can deliver widgets at a penny less per piece than the company is currently paying. That can be a sizable amount of money at the end of the year, but it may not be important to the client. Perhaps they've initiated this search for a new resource because the existing supplier has been delivering flawed widgets.

So you'll likely want to stress your flawless quality control, which delivers perfect widgets 99.9 percent of the time. It's important to remember that there are two parts to every presentation. There's the message that you want to get out and there's the message that your audience wants to hear. A great presentation is somewhere in the middle.

Typically you'll begin your presentation with some statement that tells those listening to you why it is important that they continue to pay full attention to your words. It might be something like:

There are a lot of things I can—and will—talk to you about today. But I think what I'm most proud of is that XYZ Corporation has developed a manufacturing process that turns out perfect widgets virtually 100 percent of the time. We've coupled that with a quality control system that catches any flawed widgets before they're delivered to customers. That we don't have to deal with returns saves us a bundle—a cost savings we pass on to you. So not only do you get a great product, you also get it at less cost.

If that was the way the presentation you were listening to began, you'd stay tuned in, wouldn't you? I know I would.

In part two of the presentation, you'll talk a little bit about what you've based this discussion on: that you've spoken to a dozen people at all levels in the organization and the first thing virtually every one of them said was "I wish we could get better widgets."

You might want to talk about your company and its long and illustrious history. How XYZ was the main widget supplier to General George Washington and that it was an XYZ widget that enabled him to emerge victorious at Yorkville.

Thus far you've spoken a lot about your company. In part three of the presentation, you need to talk a little about why what you're saying is important to your potential customer.

> Quality widgets mean less downtime in your operation. It means your production lines can continue to run uninterrupted by defective supplies. Less downtime equals more efficient operations, which equals greater profits.

And, finally in part four you cover all the details—pricing, delivery, discounts—that you need to fill in. You also ask for questions and finish with a conclusion. Thank you and a summation—or better still a resolution of what the next step will be. In terms of the question-and-answer part of your session, a lot of times no one wants to be the first person to ask a question. They're always afraid they'll ask a silly question and no one wants to look stupid in front of their peers or—shudder—their boss.

So what I do if no one raises their hand is ask myself questions. "I know what you want to know," I tell them. "How can I deliver everything I've promised at this phenomenally low price? Can I really guarantee everything?" I answer and lighten the mood at the same time. Invariably I get questions after that.

I want to mention a couple of other things that I've always found helpful.

When I sit down to write a presentation, I try to write stories. By nature people are storytellers. In early days, that's how we passed down our history and our culture from one generation to the next. So what I try to do is frame what I have to say in terms of anecdotes and stories rather than just facts.

For example, I talk about the funny things some of my students have said over the years. This does a couple of things. First of all, it lightens the mood in the room. But as important, it reaffirms my bona fides as a teacher. Finally, the power of stories is that you can visualize them. I know at least some of those I'm addressing see me in the classroom with the people I describe. And the fact that they're putting me—at least in their mind's eye—in a classroom is a giant step forward.

Another thing I do when I sit down to prepare a presentation is to write it from the perspective of the person who'll be listening to it. To the extent that I can, I put myself in the other person's shoes. Would I buy from this presentation? What questions has the presentation left unanswered? What else do I need to know so that I can make a sound decision on this product?

Listening to the presentation through someone else's mindset allows me to plug holes I might otherwise not be aware of. And it's more than merely being sure that all the holes are plugged. I spend time considering the demographics of the group. If it, for example, is largely made up of women, I'll probably go light on sports analogies.

And before anyone starts complaining that today's women know as much about sports as most men, that might very well be true. All I can work from is my experience, and that suggests that women usually don't follow sports as closely as men do.

In the same way, if my presentation is to a senior (in age) group, I go light on hip-hop analogies. There may be some sixty-year-old who knows that 50 Cent ain't necessarily half a buck. But I prefer to go with the percentages.

It's only after the presentation is written that I even start to worry about PowerPoint slides. As a rule of thumb, you want to keep slides simple. You don't want too much text. People should be listening to you, not reading. (That's why I never print out and distribute my PowerPoint in advance. If they can read the presentation, what am I doing there?)

You want the slides to illuminate important points. You don't need to put up slides for slides' sake. And you have to be very wary of using humor. Like beauty, humor is in the eye (or in this case ear) of the beholder. What you and 8 percent of the people there believe is hilarious can easily offend the rest of the audience. And even if your humorous slide (or comment) doesn't offend them, they may just not think it's funny. There's nothing worse than bombing in the middle of a presentation.

I don't depend on default slides. I've become pretty good in manipulating PowerPoint. But if I want something special, I use an outside consultant to help me create the effect I want. If you work in a large company, you may have someone in your IT department you can call on. Your sales manager will probably be able to refer you to someone.

When I have everything complete, I take it all to my sales buddy. My sales buddy is someone who will listen to me practice my presentation and be enough of a friend to critique it for me. He'll tell me what makes sense and what doesn't. He'll ask the questions my real audience is likely to ask. And he'll be tough on me because he knows I value his criticism and that I will return the favor. Everyone needs a sales buddy. How to select one is something we'll discuss in the next section. Meanwhile, you have your presentation. Next you have to prepare to give it.

WHAT TO TAKE FROM THIS CHAPTER

1. Don't prepare your presentation in PowerPoint. Do it independently. Decide what the major points you want to make are and then transfer them to the software. This way it is easier to resist the temptation of writing a presentation to fit the software rather than making the software fit your presentation.

2. Remember, the best presentations are conversational in tone. Avoid three-dollar words and jargon. They only lead to confusion.

3. There are two parts to a great presentation—what you want to say and what your audience wants to hear. It's important to include information about your company's quality control, but that doesn't necessarily mean you need to stress it if that wasn't a major issue with previous suppliers. Always stay focused on the goal of meeting your prospective clients' needs.

4. Typically, a presentation can be divided into four major sections. It begins with an attention-getting opening statement that announces your intention. That's followed by a section about your company's ability to meet those goals. Then, you follow that with a segment about the significance of all this to your prospect company—to its bottom line, to its manufacturing, to its quality control. Finally, you summarize everything you've said and ask for the next step.

Chapter

Getting Ready to Present

Many of the "rules" I'm going to suggest in this chapter are so obvious you'll think I'm wasting my time and yours by even mentioning them. It's not even a question of being a natural-born salesperson or not. It's a matter of common sense. But I have been around for a very long time and the sad truth is that I've seen every one of these rules broken over and over again by supposedly sophisticated salespeople.

The chances are that none of the faux pas I'm going to list here will by themselves cost you a sale. But each of the rules I'm going to mention contributes to the way your prospect views you overall and judges your professionalism. Doing everything correctly adds to your luster. It makes you appear as the kind of salesperson everyone wants to deal with—and all salespeople wish they were.

For example, we all know you only get one chance to make a good first impression. I've been there when salespeople come to presentations in sports jackets, their ties askew, and their shoes unshined. I remember pointing this out to one disheveled salesman—and, by the way, it's always men who are unkempt; women seem to take greater pride in their appearance—who said look, the prospects all wear company golf shirts with the company logo on them. It's very informal here.

Well, the golf shirts are their uniform. Yours, as a salesperson, is suits and ties for men and similar business apparel for women. Standards are changing. We've become less stringent, less uptight about what we wear and where we wear it. For example, when I was a youngster, men wore ties and jackets to baseball games.

But as salespeople we don't set fashion trends. Physically, our goal is to project an image of professionalism. Companies aren't going to place million-dollar orders with people they don't respect.

Beyond that, you've gone over your presentation with your sales buddy. Now have someone go over your slides. There's nothing worse than flashing a slide on a screen that proves to a group of prospects that you are a rotten speller. It's just a minor transgression, one that we all make, but it diminishes you because it indicates that you haven't taken the time to check your work, that this presentation wasn't really that important to you.

Or—and I've seen this a lot—you use the wrong words. For example, I've had people write me that they wanted to complete the "sail." Really. I just got an e-mail from someone who wrote—and this sadly is no joke— "their is not enough time left." Of course, that's the wrong word. And in thinking about this person's brain, my inevitable conclusion is that there is no there there.

We all make mistakes. We catch some of them with spell checker, but others invariably slip by. I'm a bad typist and my salutation will frequently come out Dear Mt. Schiffman instead of Mr. (I've long felt that they put the keys on computers and typewriters far too close together, particularly the R and the T.) Errors like this one will not be caught by spell checker. And because you wrote it, you might miss it as well on rereading. Have someone else proof your writing. Again, you do not want anything to happen that will diminish your image of professionalism in a customer's mind.

More obvious stuff: Arrive early and walk through the room where you'll be making the presentation. Check the lighting and seats placement to ensure that everyone will be able to see the presentation. Also, you want to be sure that there are electrical outlets for your computer. And, in any event, I always bring a spare battery.

Ideally, you will know who is on your side well before you begin. It's always nice to have a champion in the room. But it is really important that you don't play to them or become distracted by people you think are opposed to you.

Do not ignore anyone in the room. It's easy to fall into the trap of playing up to the senior executive in attendance; but he's likely not the sole decision-maker. And even if he is, he will solicit the views of others at the presentation. For the person you've ignored, it's just as easy—if not easier—to say something negative about your product or service than something positive. It's easier to voice an opinion favoring the status quo over change. But it's also easier just to include everyone in the presentation.

I walk around the room and try to make side comments to everyone so all feel included.

This might be a good time to point out that I have made pretty much all of these mistakes at some point myself. For example, I once was presenting to a group of higher echelon executives at a company that was considering using my services. This was a *big deal*. And by *big deal*, I'm talking well over $1 million a year. And as I am delivering my well–thought out and documented presentation, I see a woman in the corner sitting with her arms folded in front of her in the classic body language position of "leave me alone."

I'd done my homework. I knew who she was and that she was going to be very influential in the decision-making process. But I had assumed going in that she was at least going to be neutral. But her posture didn't look neutral to me. And if I didn't have her on my team, I wasn't going to get the contract.

So I stopped what I was doing and said to her, "You don't seem to be buying this. Do you have any questions?"

She said no. She thought everything I said was right on target. Apparently what I misinterpreted as lack of interest or downright hostility was just the fact that she was sitting under an air conditioning vent and didn't want to get up and move during the presentation. She thought *that* would throw things off.

A final thought here: We've become a global economy. So companies that were American owned and operated have been purchased by overseas corporations. Overseas companies have branches here. Therefore it is important that as you prepare for your presentation, you make doubly certain that it is appropriate for that group.

By that I don't mean just that your sales argument is appropriate—that is, the right product at the right price at the right time—but that it is presented in a manner appropriate to that group. For one thing, you have to be aware of cultural differences. What you or I think is funny might be insulting to someone of a different nationality. It's more than just a matter of cultural sensitivities. It's not only that you might inadvertently say or do something that is insulting to someone from another country. It could be something even simpler: That a foreign born and raised executive doesn't get some reference you make.

You might assume that the whole world knows who Willie Mays or Milton Berle are, but obviously that isn't true.

In some ways that's important with American companies as well. For the longest time, the punchline to a joke my friend told as part of his presentation to clients involved the name Kareem Abdul-Jabbar. The problem is my friend kept getting older and his audiences kept getting younger and pretty soon a good percentage of the people he spoke to didn't recognize the name.

So in place of Abdul-Jabbar, my friend substituted the name Shaquille O'Neal. He's getting his laughs again, but he claims every time he tells that story now, he feels 150 years old.

The lesson remains the same: You have to be aware of all types of cultural differences, in nationality and age and perhaps even regions of countries.

Again, most of these rules won't make or break you. And if you have an exceptional proposal, perhaps you can even break all these rules and still walk away with a contract.

But I genuinely believe that in terms of your interactions with your clients, there's a cumulative effect to the image you create. If you come in to your first meeting looking less than professional, then the first prospect you meet—the one you made the cold call on originally—is not going to move you on to the next person in the process, because you become a reflection of him.

If you tell off-color jokes, the first prospect you meet—the one you made the cold call on originally—is not going to move you on to the next person in the process, because you become a reflection of him.

He doesn't want the vice president of sales to call him and complain about your behavior. "Why did you tell that guy to call me? I wouldn't do business with that jerk if you paid me."

No one wants to get that call.

WHAT TO TAKE FROM THIS CHAPTER

1. There are (I would like to think) obvious rules of business etiquette to which you must adhere. Dress properly; you're not going for a day at the beach. Be politically correct. Making off-color comments or remarks that are generally considered offensive—even if you intend them as a joke—will hurt your cause.

2. Make sure your references are appropriate for your audience. If, for example, you are presenting to an audience of Japanese business people, referring to something particularly American might just go over their heads. Similarly, if the people you are presenting to are older, making reference to 50 Cent (or Fiddy, as I call him) is likely inappropriate.

3. Don't become distracted by people in the room giving off apparently negative vibes. You might be misinterpreting them. But even if you are right, there's nothing you can do about it.

Chapter

Closing the Sale

The sad truth of the matter is that most salespeople have one meeting, or maybe two meetings, with a potential client and then send in a proposal. Sadly, that salesman will get a certain number of orders, thus encouraging him to continue in this manner. But what he doesn't realize is that a beggar standing on a busy street with his hand out will get a certain number of alms. To me, that's not sales; that's order taking, and it illustrates the difference between the natural born and the rest of us.

The natural born is not afraid to go out and do the work. Moreover, confident that she's dotted every I and crossed every T, she's not afraid to ask for the order.

Of course, it's a lot easier to ask for an order if you know you've done the necessary prep work. There's a direct relationship between the amount of effort you've put into a project and the likelihood that you'll receive an order at the end of it.

Certainly I understand why many, if not most, salespeople are afraid of taking that final step, of actually *asking* for the sale. Traditionally, we sales folks have taken a subservient role. We watched everything we said and did, fearful we might say or do the wrong thing at the wrong time and jeopardize the order.

We don't want to seem pushy; that's just a nasty stereotype. Beyond that, I believe there's also a subtle psychological factor at play. We tend to think that if you push and get a no, it's all over. As long as there's a possibility of a sale, we can still fantasize about it, counting the commission in our dreams. However, if we ask for a sale and are turned down, both our dreams and reality are shattered. But all of this is just mental masturbation, pardon my French.

The process has become a lot more sophisticated than it was in the *Death of a Salesman* days.

In today's global economy, you can't just glad-hand prospects, give them a cigar, and take them out for drinks. For a sale to succeed in the twenty-first century, you and your prospect must be partners in the venture. He has to be vested in you and your product, because by approving the purchase he is putting himself on the line. If you don't deliver what you promise when you promise it, you will tarnish the prospect's reputation as well as yours.

Also, one of the most important mantras in my books and classes is that the more complex the sale, the bigger the sale, the more the prospect has to help you and participate. So why wouldn't you ask your partner for the order?

But you know what a lot of salespeople do? Instead of being straightforward about it, they employ little tricks I assume they believe that they're being clever. They'll take out a pen and poll it to the prospect and say something like: "As long as you've got the pen in your hand, why don't you sign the order?"

Another one of my least favorite tricks is one I call "the assumptive close." That is they'll say "On the assumption this sale is going to happen, why don't we write up the order now." If you've done the work, you don't have to *assume* that the sale will happen—it *will* happen. You don't have to do tricks or jump through hoops to get the sale; the straightforward approach is always best.

Let's start off by making the basic assumption that not only have you done your homework, but you've done it correctly. You've spoken to the right people. You're offering the right product or service at the right price. And the timetable is right—you'll be able to deliver at the right time and to the right place. Then it is perfectly acceptable to simply say: "I've looked at this proposal from every angle. I've discussed it with a number of you. And I think it makes a great deal of sense. Before I came here, I checked my warehouse and we have enough M49 in stock that we can start shipping to you almost immediately. All I need is your okay to get the ball rolling."

Some of you may be shocked by that. The conventional wisdom is that salespeople aren't entitled to have opinions, or if they have one, they aren't allowed to express it. But that's not true.

Consider a recent experience I had. I made a sales call at a company where I'd been highly recommended. The people I met with actually tried to sell me. They told me what problems they had with their sales force. They were familiar with a particular program I run and believed that it could solve those problems. They wanted to schedule something immediately.

But something seemed wrong to me. I asked them for a little bit of time to allow me to look into their operation. What I saw was different from what they saw. I came back to the prospects and (diplomatically) told them they were wrong. That a different series of classes I offered would work better for them. And I was right.

A number of you might say, "Idiot, you had the sale. Why take a chance and screw it up? Wasn't it presumptuous of you to voice your opinion when those executives clearly knew their company better than you did?"

My feeling is why can't you say that? Where is it written that the salesperson isn't an expert? Where is it written that a salesperson can't have an opinion? Your expertise is what you bring to the table. Otherwise these companies would just consult a book or a computer when deciding what to order.

Okay, then, the presentation is over. You ask for the business. Depending upon the size of the order and the size of the company, you will likely get a yes right then or a definitive timetable for when you'll get an answer. What happens if you get a "no"?

There might be some internal political factor at play you were unaware of. Or a new element could have been added to the mix—someone transferred from elsewhere or was newly hired and inserted himself into the process at the last second.

But more likely, if you get a negative response, the chances are that you got something wrong. You didn't speak to the right person, your terms were not the best, or your timing was bad. It might be that in coming up with your proposal you spent too much time negotiating with yourself and not enough with the client.

But all is not lost. If you've put in the time and effort and presumably built a relationship with the prospect, you have every right to go back and ask what happened. You can literally say that—"What happened?"—and put it on a personal level. You've just taken a big hit after putting in a massive effort with your prospect's help. A lot of sales training programs make a point to remind you that a rejection is business, not personal. That all you should do is move on to the next client. I disagree. If you don't have enough of yourself vested in your sales effort then you're not doing the job. It is personal. By rejecting your effort and ideas, they're rejecting you. And you should be angry.

Very angry and very diplomatic. And if you ask the question the right way, you will get an answer. *But you have to ask the question.* You've already lost the sale, so what have you got to lose? It may turn out to be something that is easily fixable. You missed an element in your research. You didn't get to all the right people.

When you ask what went wrong, at least you will get resolution of some kind. And you will get (and I hate this term) closure. If it is something that can't be fixed, you won't waste more time fretting. If it is something that can be fixed, you can find out how soon you can come back.

And where there's life, there's hope.

WHAT TO TAKE FROM THIS CHAPTER

1. There is nothing wrong with asking for an order. You've done the work. You are entitled to resolution.

2. Take it personally. You've put in substantial effort on this project and presumably had verification of your work at every step. It's okay to ask what went wrong. If you made a mistake, you may be able to correct it. But even if it's too late to make things right, you'll walk away with a valuable lesson. Painful, but valuable because you'll never make the same mistake again.

Chapter 22

Managing Accounts

There are two sides to every coin. In sales, it's heads you get new business and tails you retain existing accounts. And sometimes it's funny how your perspective changes.

We spend most of our lives pitching new business. We make cold calls. We study a prospective client's business. We make proposals. We make presentations. And hopefully we get the business.

But how often do we ask ourselves *why* we got the business. What happened at the company that allowed us to get our foot in the door? Remember, I've said our biggest hurdle isn't the competition; our greatest obstacle to success is inertia on the part of the client.

The reality is that getting in the door is always a problem. You may feel you have a better product or better price or better service or better quality or better whatever, and you try—unsuccessfully—to get an audience. Still you get "thanks, but no thanks." If you are passionate about what you do—and I assume you are—rejection is enough to get you angry. However, if you step back for a second and look at the situation objectively, you can *sort of* understand the logic behind the brushoff.

Why Start Trouble?

More often than not, the people responsible for buying decisions and their minions are in a comfort zone. That is, the widgets they need are being delivered on time. They work well enough that no one on the factory floor is complaining about quality problems. They're priced reasonably enough so that no one from accounting is jabbering on the phone about high material costs. So why see a salesperson and risk upsetting the apple cart? Why unnecessarily introduce a new factor into the equation? From the prospect's perspective, all you can bring to the table is trouble. Suppose your product is better or cheaper or whatever—it raises the question of how come they weren't on board years earlier. No, it's better and simpler to let sleeping dogs lie. (See a couple of paragraphs down for a different perspective.)

So why is it that you do get appointments and do sell against entrenched suppliers? Ironically, it's usually because of inertia. The same inertia that is your enemy when it comes to your prospects is your friend when it comes to your competition. It's easy to get lazy with a long-standing client, one you're convinced you'll be carrying on your books forever.

Look, we've all become complacent. The company is responsible for a steady income flowing to your personal coffers. But time is at a premium. You start to woo other accounts with the fervor and devotion you once lavished on this account. Your attention is focused on generating new business. Weekly luncheons with your contacts become every-other-week-affairs. And then that drifts down to maybe once a month.

Essentially, what you are unwittingly doing is opening the door for someone else to come in and snatch all or part of this business from you. A division of this company starts a new product manufacturing line that needs widgets. The buyer doesn't think of you because he doesn't know you or you're just not around. The division you work for introduces a new product that requires something other than widgets that your company sells. But you're not there when they're planning this, so someone else gets the order. As much as you and your bosses want you to mine new business remember this:

An account in the hand is worth two in the bush.

In the same amount of time and using less effort, you almost always have the opportunity to get more business from existing accounts than new accounts are likely to generate. I realize that's a broad brush statement and is far from absolute. New accounts can greatly increase your income. But, in terms of the amount of effort you have to put in and *as a general rule*, mining existing accounts is more profitable than new ones. You are already well established in the company. You and your product or service are known commodities. Why wouldn't they stay with you? (See what I mean about different perspectives?)

So you say to me, "Steve, you've just spent a lot of time telling us how important it is to spend part of each day cold calling and how to get new accounts. Now you're saying don't bother."

No, that's not what I'm saying. I'm saying that you have to strike a balance between managing existing accounts and seeking new ones. You can't forget to pay attention to existing accounts and mine them for new business. On the one hand, accounts mature. Companies merge. People are let go, retire, change jobs. And then what happens? If you don't have new business to fall back on, you're out in the cold.

A lot of what I teach comes from personal experience; in this case specifically there are lessons I learned the hard way. Twice. I've had accounts that were keeping me in the finer things in life. I'm not talking Porsche or anything like that. But I am talking long weekends. Extra vacations. I took advantage of a situation and wasn't aware of some changes that had occurred—changes critical to the client's business and, as it turned out, my own. And twice I paid the price. Once I lost the account entirely and another time the amount of business I did with the customer was sharply reduced. Suddenly I found myself scrambling for business.

So I learned. Yes, I constantly search for new business. I am on the phone every morning in my office. But what I don't do is allow my pursuit of new business to interfere with servicing existing accounts.

Let me give you a few examples of what I mean. A saleswoman, Barbara, landed my company as an account. We used the binding equipment she sold for our proposals and workbooks. She developed a good rapport with us, and while we weren't her largest account, we provided a steady stream of business.

All of a sudden she stopped calling us. When we called her, she was quick to fulfill our requests. But we were growing. We were tired of the look of the books and the amount of time the staff had to take to produce them. I'd opened a distribution system, hired four new people, and was looking for ways to introduce efficiency.

One afternoon Barbara came in to see if we needed our regular $100 order and was shocked to see the changes we'd introduced. She wanted to know why we didn't call her. She said she could have helped.

I didn't call her because other vendors had come in and been helpful. I didn't call her because I was unaware she had any expertise in this area. And I didn't call her because she wasn't around when we were contemplating and making the changes so she could put in her two cents. She brought in her manager and a vice president to try to win back the business. She even made up a nameplate for my desk that said: Stephan "Chief" Schiffman, thinking that might win my heart and soul. It did. But what it didn't win was any more business.

Look. I did $5,000 in business with her a year. I know it wasn't a lot, but it was steady. If anyone knows how tough a salesperson's life is, I do. So it wasn't like I expected her to come in every week. But a phone call every once in a while, to ask what's new, to see if there's anything else she can do or sell, to show that she's still interested, would have been nice.

If she had called, I might have mentioned my new project. If she had called and I was thinking about her, I might have called her when this project was in development. But she didn't and I didn't and she's the one who is out the commission.

I was a small account, but this business would have "catapulted" me up to medium. Not that that makes a difference. This kind of stuff happens with large accounts, too. My favorite story about this has to do with a guy I'll call Phil, though this situation is so unique that he (and the people who work at his company) will certainly know to whom I refer.

Phil worked for a large oil company and had just one account, a major car company we'll call Studebaker. Phil felt his job was to keep the account happy, and he apparently did. He went out there once or twice a week and did whatever he had to do. The company continued to buy lubricant additives and oil from him.

I went on a sales call with him once and he did fine with the people he saw—at least while I was there. Afterward, I asked him how many people in the company dealt with the kinds of products he sold. He guesstimated that there were 400 in about thirty groups. I asked him how many people he saw on his weekly visits. He said three. That kind of blew my mind. Here was a guy who could move around 400 people in a company he was already doing business with and pick up additional orders (for his company) and income (for himself) and he didn't do it.

I asked "Why don't you do that?" His answer, quick and short: He doesn't get paid to do that. I wasn't going to get into a discussion (argument) with him about it, but I found his answer unbelievable. Forget the fact that he was cheating himself out of potentially much more income, but expanding the business was *exactly what he was getting paid for*.

Contrast that with Jack, who works for a defense contractor. Jack was the consummate salesperson. He knew everyone at the Pentagon. He'd go in every day starting early in the morning and meet people. He was so well known there that he was invited into meetings to come up with ideas that would help these colonels devise new approaches to the problems they were working on. Now here's a guy who sold military hardware and he was asked to sit in on meetings about ideas and concepts.

So let's compare these two guys. Jack knew how to penetrate an account. He was a salesman, yes, but was considered a consultant by his customers, a resource. He'd go to these meetings where problems were discussed, think out answers on his own time, and come back with whatever solutions he came up with.

He was interested in the account. He read industry publications. He spoke to people. And he stayed ahead of the curve. So when a project came to fruition, he'd been part of the team that developed it. Obviously that gave him a better chance to win the bid. Why was he so highly thought of? Because he consistently came back to the military and said "I have an idea." "Idea" is one of the most powerful words you can use in sales. When you tell someone you have an idea for them, something that will help them perform a task better than they are currently doing, they will listen to you. And if you are consistently correct, they will respect you because you will have proved yourself to be far above the norm.

Phil was in a similar position. The auto manufacturers are always looking for new ideas. Phil's client had an appetite to absorb new business, but Phil didn't have an appetite to sell it. Perhaps he was thinking about retirement. I don't know. I don't know whether he had ideas he could have offered. But I do know that the least valuable commodity in the world is an idea not implemented. And right next to that is an idea that never gets an audience.

The question then becomes how do I penetrate the account? You do that in the same way you got the account in the first place. Remember the Power of Twelve? You asked for names. Why would you not do that again? The widget buyer in Division A may not know the widget buyer in Division B. So just follow what I call six degrees of inspiration. The day before I wrote this chapter I met with two sales managers and a district manager for a company I'd run some seminars for. We were evaluating the program (they loved it, of course), and the conversation moved to how they'd done so much better in the last quarter (thanks to my training) than the district that had traditionally led the company in sales.

Without my prompting (although I would have asked), they gave me the name of a regional manager I should contact about doing additional business with the company.

When I've asked, I've actually had someone walk me to another person's office to introduce me. But that will only happen if you are a Jack—as in Defense Department Jack—a salesperson who doesn't ignore the company just because you are already getting sales. They will only do that if you are a salesperson who makes himself a resource, part of the furniture, someone not seen as an outsider, but as a member of the team.

WHAT TO TAKE FROM THIS CHAPTER

1. Mining existing accounts is critical and potentially more profitable (in terms of time and effort) than going after new business.

2. Remember, the reason you get new business is because your prospect is dissatisfied with something the existing supplier is doing—or not doing. The potential client is so upset that he or she is willing to overcome the normal inertia that sets in when you've had a long-time supplier and go out in search of a new one. Ignoring existing clients, providing a lower level of service, and not staying in touch are all reasons a client may go out to test the supply-line waters.

3. Most people are so focused on getting new business they lose what once was their single-minded focus: those companies already paying the bills. Staying in regular touch with existing clients makes sense on a number of levels. People change. Your ally in the purchasing department may be promoted, quit, or even be fired. You need to be there when the replacement takes over. As important, companies add new product lines or need additional services. You need to be around so people will think of you when those kinds of decisions are made.

Chapter 23

Knowing When to Punt

On a business trip a couple of years ago, I got into a conversation with the gentleman sitting next to me. We started out talking about sports and then moved on to business. It turns out he is the vice president of sales for a large international printing company, with an extensive background in sales.

I of course am the head of a large sales training organization with an extensive background in diplomatically switching any number of conversations into a sales pitch. So here we were; a match made in heaven.

I gently brought our discussion around to training, told him a little about my philosophy, and waited to gauge his reaction. He jumped on board immediately. Yes, we can definitely use that. Neither of us had business cards immediately available, so I wrote down his e-mail address and promised to contact him with more information.

I dropped him a brief note a couple of days later, but didn't get a response. I figured that the dog ate his e-mail before he had a chance to read it. (It's pitiful, isn't it, how falsely optimistic sales reps are in pursuit of a contract?) So I sent another.

I still hadn't received a reply about three weeks later, so I looked his company up on the Web, found his telephone number, and called. He wasn't there so I left a message. But I still didn't hear a peep from him. I figured the dog ate his voice mail. So I called again. This time I got him in. Oh, of course he remembered me. He'd just been busy, and hadn't had an opportunity to get back to me. He was off to a meeting, but definitely would call me back later that afternoon. Definitely.

Of course, I never heard from him. Two diametrically opposite emotions flowed through my body—anger and happiness. The reason for my anger was obvious. It bothered me that this guy didn't have the courtesy to tell me he wasn't interested. I know people don't like to deliver bad news, but there were so many places he could have stopped this.

I'd Learned My Lesson!

He could have answered my first e-mail and said he checked when he got back and there was no budget for training. Or he might have said that his boss decided this was not the time to do sales training. Or he just could have told me the truth—when he got back to his office he'd thought about it and decided he wasn't interested. A simple "I'm sorry" would have been sufficient.

What made this worse was that he was a salesman. He'd spent a career lifetime trying to connect to people who did the same lousy thing. You'd think he'd have a little more sympathy for fellow sales reps. You'd think.

That explains my anger, but what, you ask, could I possibly be happy about? Simple: I never called him again. It's a lesson I learned from a natural born I worked with early on in my career. When I first got into the business my mantra was only no means no. Yes means yes. And no response means there's still life, and I have a shot at a deal. A colleague saw and heard me (he sat at the desk next to mine) going after this small piece of business week after week. Every Wednesday morning, he'd come in with an extra cup of coffee for me and ask, "isn't today 'Joe Day?'" (Wednesday morning is when I called to touch base with the elusive prospect.)

He could see—frankly it was obvious, everyone could see—that I was becoming increasingly frustrated. Finally, he couldn't take it anymore. Instead of bringing me a cup of coffee, he took me out. His message: "Sometimes the only way to make the pain go away is to stop banging your head against the wall." And he was right.

The only small consolation I had was that I wasn't the only salesperson who walks around falsely optimistic. Here's another story from a sales rep I worked with, Bill, who told me about a prospect he worked on for several months. Interestingly enough, the initial sales call came from the prospect, Frank, asking for information on what the company provided. And Frank claimed he was in a rush to move forward.

The call came late on a Friday afternoon, so Bill immediately went into overdrive to provide what the prospect needed. He didn't overwhelm Frank; don't interpret it that way. He just sent Frank some sales material, letters of recommendation from several clients, and a covering letter urging the prospect to get in touch if he needed anything else. If he hadn't heard from Frank before then, Bill would call the prospect the following Wednesday, as they'd agreed during their phone conversation.

Bill is nothing if not thorough. He put the package together in time for a FedEx pickup. But when he got home he thought about some other details that would help him make his case. So he went back to the office on Saturday and e-mailed some additional information. And then he waited.

When he didn't hear anything further by Wednesday, Bill called to discuss what the next step would be. Surprise: The prospect barely remembered his name. As for that sense of urgency, from the initial call; it dissipated. He hadn't bothered to look at the material that was mailed, print out what was e-mailed, or study anything.

As you might imagine, it was quite disheartening for Bill. But just when he resigned himself to moving on, the prospect, Frank, urged the rep to call back the following Monday. "I'll let you know what we think then."

To me, that's a buying signal if there ever was one. It turned out, however, that it was just another false alarm. When Bill called on Monday, Frank told him that they were looking at other companies and hadn't even gotten to look at his material yet. But, he added, "don't be put off, because persistence is the key to selling."

Frank is right, to a point. Persistence is important. Even the worst sales rep will pick up some business merely by being persistent. In other words, if you pester someone enough, they'll throw a bone your way. But is that business worth having?

Does it make sense to go after someone month after month when you are no better off, no closer to a contract in month nine than you were in month one? The answer clearly is no.

Believe it or not, there are appropriate times in the sales environment to say no. When is that time? There is no single answer for everyone. It depends on you. It depends on the customer. It depends on how many hoops he tries to make you jump through. And it depends on your tolerance for humiliation.

Two Principles Involved

For some buyers, it's all about the power to make salespeople sweat. Obviously, some sales cycles take longer than others. Obviously, you will be more persistent with a potential $10 million account than you will with a $500 account. But the principles are the same:

▶ How many hoops do you want to jump through for this sale? Are you making enough progress—are you making any progress—that indicates you should continue your quest? Or are you Don Quixote, tilting at windmills and imaginary sales opportunities?

▶ Can your time be better spent elsewhere? Does it make sense to continue down this apparently dead-end street, or should you back out and get back on Opportunity Highway?

▶ If you get any business from these accounts, is it worth having? If they're making you jump through hoops now, what will they make you do to keep the business?

I really believe in persistence, but in a real-world way. My experience is that the longer you go after an account, the less likely it is to happen.

WHAT TO TAKE FROM THIS CHAPTER

1. Even in a sales environment, there comes a time when you have to say "no" to a prospect: No more jumping through hoops; no more being at your beck and call 24/7; no more spending my valuable time gathering more and more information from you. You've had enough time to make up your mind.

2. "No" time varies from customer to customer and sales rep to sales rep. There is no single answer for everyone. It has to do with the size of the potential order, the length of the typical sales cycle, and the sales rep's tolerance for pain and humiliation.

3. The sales rep also has to ask if the time spent pursuing the impossible dream sale might be better spent elsewhere, nurturing existing accounts or cold calling on potential new ones.

4. Also, is the account even worth having? At some point, servicing an account just isn't worth it in terms of your mental and emotional health.

5. Yes, persistence is a good thing. But only to the point of diminishing returns.

Chapter 24

Asking and Answering Questions

The prevailing wisdom in our business is that the key to success in sales is the ability to listen. I can't tell you how many times managers have called and asked me for help because their reps "just don't know how to listen." Unfortunately, I can't provide the kind of assistance they're looking for; I feel this is one instance where the prevailing wisdom is wrong.

The problem isn't that the salespeople don't listen. It's that they don't give prospects an opportunity to say something worth listening to. All too often, a salesperson comes in, offers a perfunctory greeting, and moves right into a standard pitch. That doesn't work well.

The reality is that meeting someone for the first time in a business setting is really not much different from meeting someone in a social setting. Usually, when two people initially meet there's a scrim barrier between them. Let's say you and another party-goer are introduced by the host. You shake hands and if one of you doesn't initiate an interesting conversation, somehow raise that curtain, both of you will move on to someone else.

Frankly, starting that conversation is something that natural borns are really good at. They tend to be glib, make small talk easily, and always seem able to come up with witty and insightful repartee.

Raising the Level of Conversation

Obviously, not everyone has that gift of gab. I know I didn't when I started out in sales. But that was probably because I was young. I was still awkward in social situations so clearly that was going to carry over to social-cum-business situations. But over the course of time I learned some very important lessons. In many ways, these lessons enabled me to become a better salesperson—and, in effect, changed my life.

First, there are different levels of conversation. For our purposes, the most structured, most formal, most unappealing is the business conversation, the one described above that moves from hello to pitch in one quick step. It is stiff and stilted and as often as not leaves your prospect with his guard up throughout the meeting.

Social conversations are at a higher level and your goal as a sales rep is to try to make a business conversation social in nature. Social conversations are more relaxed, and they allow your prospect to relax and lower his guard. In the process, he's likely to give you the information you need.

But don't confuse the situation in your head. Your goal here isn't to win a friend. You just want a good and *mutually-profitable* business relationship. So you have to keep control of the discussion and propel it in the direction you want to go.

Another important point that I've made at least twice before but is worth repeating is that we all tend to talk in stories. It's part of the human condition and the way that knowledge and memories were passed down from generation to generation.

Also, people love to talk about themselves.

Finally, people respond in kind. So if you say "good morning," they'll respond "good morning." They won't say, "My wife's name is Jill." That means people are relatively easy to guide through a conversation. And it is your job to get the conversation going and guide it.

The best way to do that is by asking questions. I've covered this topic briefly in an earlier chapter, but I consider it so sufficiently important that it warrants its own chapter.

We all have our standard opening gambits, and what works for me won't necessarily work for you. But just to give you an idea of how simple this can be, if I'm at a cocktail party (business or social) and don't know anyone, I've become the opposite of shy. (Un-shy?) I'll go over to any number of people and introduce myself. "Hi, my name is Steve Schiffman."

They'll invariably respond in kind, something like: "Hi, Bill Smith."

"Bill?'

"Yes, Bill."

Now I've heard the name three times, him to me, me to him, and then again when he confirms it. Then I ask what they do for a living, and almost always the conversation starts flowing. (By the way it works well whether I introduce myself or someone introduces the two of us.)

Be Sincerely Sincere

It wasn't exactly an epiphany, but at some point I became comfortable doing that, and realized how simple it would be to transfer that comfort level to a cold call. Clearly, since I've called for an appointment, I know the person's name and what he does. But the principle is the same.

I might start off: "You know, everyone I've spoken to says this is a great company to work for. How long have you worked here?"

Depending upon his answer, I'll ask how long he's been in this job, how he got it, and how he enjoys it. Whatever story he tells you will trigger more questions. A couple of points here:

▶ First, you really have to pay attention to the prospect's responses—and you really ought to care what he or she has to say. The natural-born salesperson shows empathy. Showing someone you are really interested in them will open them up. George Burns said, "The secret of acting is sincerity. If you can fake that, you've got it made." If you can fake sincerity, more power to you. But I have the feeling since you are a sales pro and care enough about your job to read this book, you already are the type of person who cares about people. Not necessarily in a Barbra Streisand way, but in a way that you are genuinely curious about them and what they do.

▶ Second, remember, I was pretty far along in my career before I figured out how to make these conversations work. This is a skill that can be learned. And it takes patience.

I was on a sales call in Texas, and I did exactly what I just told you, but the prospect wasn't cooperating. I guess he didn't know about the need for him to tell stories, because all I got were short, clipped answers. But I refused to give up easily. I knew he'd just joined the company from elsewhere, so I asked how long he'd been in Dallas.

That changed the entire tenor of the conversation. He'd just moved from Florida and loved Dallas. He told me about the townhouse he purchased. His entire body relaxed, and I was soon able to get the information from him that I came for.

There comes a time, though, when you have to move the conversation from personal to professional. Remember, it's not just about listening to what they have to say, but asking the right questions that allow them to give you useful answers.

One question leads naturally to another. I'll ask how a company got started. I did that recently and got a forty-five-minute response from an eager executive who went on to purchase my sales training. How leads to why. And that can lead to a discussion about products and product development. So it's not just asking a question. It's starting a two-way conversation.

WHAT TO TAKE FROM THIS CHAPTER

1. Natural-born sales reps have the ability to raise the level of a discussion from mundane business talk to an interesting business-related conversation. But this is a skill that easily can be mastered with practice.

2. It's not about listening, as many sales managers believe. It's about asking questions that elicit answers worth listening to.

3. People talk in stories—if you give them a chance. Don't ask questions that can be answered with a simple "yes" or "no." Give them a shot at storytelling.

4. People respond in kind. If you say "hello," they'll say "hello." If you ask them how they got their job, they'll tell you. It may start off slowly, but lob in enough story balls, and the prospect will hit one out of the park—and then tell you the story of how she did it.

5. Once you bridge the gap from sales call to conversation, the prospects let their guard down and everything becomes much easier and more relaxed.

6. It's important that you be genuinely interested in what the prospect has to say—or be able to fake interest.

Chapter

Finding Allies

A lot of companies proudly proclaim that they have "sales teams." More often than not, though, that's just marketing blather. You and I know the truth, don't we? Selling is an individual sport. One of the attributes that make great sales reps is competitiveness, the need to win. Help? Heck, we don't need help. We do it alone!

Not so the natural-born salespeople I've known. They understand that selling is a form of warfare. And even the strongest sales rep sometimes needs allies in battle. In fact, natural borns actively pursue alliances, both in the (potential) client companies and in their own organizations, as though they were on *Survivor*—which, in a sense, they are. The natural borns recognize that the more people they have on their side, the better their chances of clinching a sale.

Let's talk first about finding allies in your prospect company. What do I mean by that? Certainly, it's possible to go into a company, do a minimal amount of research, and come away with a signed contract. But those opportunities are rarer and rarer, in part because there are very few products or services that are unique. Not every product or service is a commodity, of course, but usually there are two or three suppliers for every item.

That's true for your client company, too, which undoubtedly is facing increased competition from others in this great new global economy. So they're taking harder, closer looks at their suppliers (you) and evaluating them more stringently.

What does all this mean for you? Going back to the metaphor about war, you need to be armed to the gills. Part of that armor is information. The Power of Twelve is one way you arm yourself with information about the company. But it is also a great vehicle to recruit allies who will guide you deep into enemy territory. (Okay, I'm getting carried away with these allusions to war and battle, but you get the idea, don't you?)

Here are some examples from my own personal experience to illustrate what I mean. I was hoping to sell a series of my courses and my initial contact was a person in charge of training in the company's HR department. She was the prime decision-maker, though she always consulted with her colleagues.

Going by the book (which I happen to have written) I said to her, "Before I make a proposal I'd like to get a better feel for how your company's sales force works in the field. Can you arrange for me to speak to some of your sales reps, so I can see how they operate in the real world? I'd also like to spend some time with some of your sales executives. This way, I'll be able to put something far more intelligent in front of you."

I thought she'd say okay, because our meeting had gone pretty well. However, she was not warm to the idea. She said she'd have to get clearance, and I expected that was the end of things. But a few days later, she asked me to call the regional vice president of sales and speak to him.

I of course did as I was told, and arranged an appointment with, let's call him James. I explained what I do and he immediately got excited. He said he's tried unsuccessfully for the last three years to introduce this type of course at the company. The stumbling block was the head of HR, who wasn't a fan of any kind of training.

He picked up the phone right there in front of me, called his boss, the vice president of sales, explained what was going on, and the two of them ultimately arranged a meeting for the three of us and the senior vice president of marketing the following week.

They all liked the ideas I proposed and ultimately insisted on attending my formal presentation to the HR department. They were so vociferous in their support at the presentation that there was really no way I could be denied the contract.

Frankly, this doesn't happen often—this way. But it does happen. And if you do what's expected of you, you'll have an ally for life. For example:

A company I've worked with in the past recently decided to hire an entirely new sales force for a product launch. I knew this company. I knew its culture. In fact, I knew everything except how to guarantee that I got a "yes."

So the first thing I did was bounce my idea off the company's CFO, an ally from a previous sale. He thought my suggestions were "brilliant" (his word, not mine—but who am I to disagree?) and went on to tell me exactly what I had to do to win the contract. His instructions were very specific: He told me the criteria that would be used to select the trainer, how to price my bid, and how to position myself.

Not only did he do that, but then he called the CEO in and the three of us discussed the project. The only one left to convince was the president, and when we met he was outnumbered three-to-one.

In both of these examples, the people who helped me out were high-ranking executives. But your allies don't have to be. The most important thing is that you find people who see the wisdom of what you are trying to accomplish. Even when they are not decision-makers themselves, they can guide you through the labyrinth corridors of politics and intrigue.

But even if they can't do that now, they may be able to sometime in the future. You need to nurture and cherish them. The sad fact is that in the business world, as in life, the number of people who get you and what you are trying to accomplish is dwarfed by people who have their own agendas and don't care about you at all.

I don't mean you should manipulate allies to do your bidding. Instead, what you should be doing is building a relationship where they trust you because they know you'll walk away from a deal if it isn't right.

In-house is a little different. You're on your own most of the time, but even the finest honed athlete needs a coach. You need to find someone in the company who can help you in a couple of areas.

The first is obvious: you need someone to bounce your ideas off of. "This is my situation. I've discovered this and this about the company. Here's what I propose. What do you think?"

Your ally may have a different take on things and looking at the same situation with a different pair of eyes may see an alternative solution. Not necessarily a better one. That's for you to decide. But another viewpoint may cause you to alter your thinking.

My experience is that sometimes sales reps get overwhelmed at the complexity of their own sale, when it isn't actually as involved as they believe it to be. So it helps to get someone else's perspective.

And you may not even need to get his or her advice. My own personal experience is that I most want to get someone else involved when subconsciously I sense that something is wrong, that I am not going down the right road. I've learned if I can't explain it succinctly to a colleague, something is wrong. I don't have enough information; I haven't thought through the information properly or there is some other basic flaw in my concept.

Whenever that happens, I know the sale isn't going to take place, because there's something blocking me. Other eyes provide additional peripheral vision to help me see the sale—and the road that will get me there.

On perhaps a seemingly less important but equally critical note, you need someone to look over your presentation, to check spelling and grammar, to be sure you don't make a silly (stupid?) mistake that casts you and the company in a bad eye.

Frankly, the person who should be doing this is the sales manager. Technically, that's his or her job. But if for whatever reason your manager is not able to help or up to it, you have to find someone else. What typically occurs is that you pair off with a friend in the office, someone you trust, someone you have a bond with. And that often works.

But I have an alternative suggestion. Don't pair off with your friend. Pick the meanest S.O.B. in your office; someone no one likes. You don't need a friend in this situation. You need someone who will have no qualms about criticizing you, someone who won't be afraid to ask you tough questions (in the same way a client might), and someone who will really test you and your plan.

WHAT TO TAKE FROM THIS CHAPTER

1. Even the most independent salesperson needs help. It's better than okay—it's to your advantage—to find allies in your prospect company.

2. Who are your allies? These are people who see the wisdom of what you are trying to sell and the rationale you are using to sell it.

3. They don't need to be decision-makers to be valuable allies. It can be a lower-level employee who explains how decisions are made and the idiosyncrasies of some of the people involved; this is valuable information that enables you to hone your presentation.

4. An ally in your company can be just as helpful. Another pair of eyes examining—and proofreading—your presentation can alert you to problems and wrong turns you might not have noticed on your own.

5. Reviewing a proposal with an internal ally forces you to concentrate on exactly what points you want to get across. If you cannot explain them satisfactorily to a colleague, you won't be able to explain them to a client.

6. Don't pick a friend to be your internal ally. A friend may be reluctant to criticize you and point out even gaping holes in your proposal. Bounce your ideas off the meanest S.O.B. in your office; he'll give you an honest reaction.

Chapter 26

Lessons from a Cabbie

I **was** in a cab perhaps thirty years ago when I noticed that the driver had some kind of a chart with pushpins in it. As I sat down and told him my destination, he moved one of the pushpins—igniting my curiosity.

I asked him about it and he said his goal was to work only nine months a year, and he'd calculated to the day what he had to earn to get three months off. He figured out his average fare and his average tip. He kept accurate track of his earnings, and worked enough to meet his daily earnings goal.

Every time he picked up a fare (this being an age well before the laptop) he moved his push pins around. In doing so, he also figured out what were the most productive days of the week and what were the most productive hours in the day. He knew where he could find the most productive customers, what the best days to take off were, and even what the best hour to take a break was.

It was a surprisingly sophisticated system that varied by the seasons. During most of the year, he worked the midtown and financial areas in Manhattan trolling for business people. Trips generally were short and tips were high. During the summer, when a lot of New Yorkers were on vacation, he worked tourist areas and hotels. Trips were longer, but his banter and knowledge of New York City encouraged generosity.

Unlike a lot of taxi drivers, who'd run out to the airport, sit for an hour hoping to snag a big trip, this driver made it his business to know where the best business was and to go out and pursue it.

Are you beginning to see the moral of this tale? If you're a gambler, you don't go on vacation to Iowa or Montana. You visit Atlantic City, Las Vegas, or the nearest casino. Like the cabbie, you need to go where the action is instead of sitting by the phone waiting for sales to magically flow in.

As a salesperson, you ultimately control your annual compensation. You know who your best customers are and who your potential best customers are. The only thing that limits you is time—or, more accurately, lack of it. There are just so many hours in the day, there are just so many miles you can drive, so many passengers you can pick up. There are just so many hours you can work, because your prospect isn't going to be in the office at two in the morning waiting for your call.

I believe there is a perception that the more hours you work, the more money you'll make. That isn't necessarily true. Making bucks isn't a function of long hours, but of selling smart.

It's not a bad idea to emulate the cab driver and figure out how much money you want to make to achieve whatever your goals are. Once you get that figure, narrow it down to what you need to earn every day, every hour to meet that goal.

That's how much your time is worth. Just to make the math easier, let's say you need $104,000 a year to live the lifestyle you want (and deserve). That's two grand a week, four hundred bucks a day, or $50 an hour. Does it pay, then, to spend two or three days a week keeping an account that generates only a few hundred dollars a year in commission?

I remember that in one of my early jobs I replaced a gifted salesperson. This guy was brilliant. Everyone loved him and wondered if I'd be able to maintain his accounts at the level they were for him—especially since he was off to a competitor. I, on the other hand, was young, eager, and stupid. Not only was I planning on maintaining his current level of business, I was going to break new accounts.

I went over his account list and started making calls. I concentrated on the most promising to an extent that would have driven a time management expert to distraction. Ultimately I landed a piece of their business. But when I figured it out, at the end of the year I worked that account for about $1.50 an hour. And it became worse once they were clients. Nothing I did or arranged was satisfactory. A few months later, I ran into my predecessor at a conference and told him my experience. He just laughed.

"I knew early on that those guys were pains in the [neck]," he said—though neck wasn't the word he used. "I didn't have time for that. I had more important fish to fry."

It was a valuable lesson. It made me realize early on in my career that it's okay to fire an account if it's not profitable. There is no need to keep banging your head against a wall. Your sales manager might not like that idea; if she has a problem, let her pass the account on to someone else. Or better still, keep the account but only put in the amount of time it's worth.

By that I don't mean you automatically reject a small account. Those giant oak trees were once tiny seedlings. It's like a stock. You find a company with potential, you put it in your portfolio. But you have another company that seems to be heading nowhere, get rid of it. That investment can better be used elsewhere.

You have to know where that "elsewhere" is. It takes time and experience, but if you pay attention like the cab driver, you'll know where those customers are and when they'll be there.

Finally, there are two words in the phrase "work smart." It's still work. Otherwise they'd call it vacation. No matter how smart you are, you have to put in the time and effort. There are no quick answers, no shortcuts.

WHAT TO TAKE FROM THIS CHAPTER

1. The only limit to success is time. There are just so many hours in the day. You have to put them to the best use.
2. Decide what your time is worth, and try only to pursue accounts worth your time.
3. If an account asks more of your time than it is worth (now and in the foreseeable future), fire it. Either give it to someone lower than you on the totem pole (who may be grateful for the added income) or just pay enough attention to the account that it at least comes close to paying its own way.
4. Small accounts with potential are exempt from rule number three.
5. Working smart doesn't mean you can slack off on your effort. Otherwise they'd call it vacationing smart. You still have to put in the time.

Chapter 27

Drop the Turtle Attitude

For the last thirty years, I've lined my desk and the shelves in my office with little statues of turtles. It serves as a reminder to me of another office I was in, that of a prospect of a large *Fortune* 500 company.

He had turtles, too, and just to make small talk (I wasn't really interested) I asked him about the significance of his reptilian fascination. He said it was something he saw in an office years earlier—a plaque that said in order to get anywhere a turtle has to stick its neck out.

He thought that was pretty much right on target, and began collecting little turtles as a reminder to fight complacency. And I did, too.

To me, the turtle represents the very real fear a lot of salespeople have of taking risks. I believe that's more than a little ironic, since getting into a sales career—where income can swing wildly from year to year—is something of a risk. But my experience is that too many of you prefer to play it safe, when being just a little crazy can substantially improve your performance—and your finances.

I'm not saying that risk necessarily equals success. But I do believe that a no-risk approach to selling definitely will not lead to success. But there are levels of risk. Some risk-taking is acceptable. Some is too much, uh, risk, that's the word I'm looking for.

The best analogy I can make is to the gamblers on the televised no-limit hold 'em shows. If you watch them as I do you'll see that they know the odds of every move they make. If he sees the other person's hand (as in an all-in situation) one will say to the other, "You're a three-to-two favorite," because they know the percentages—probably down to the third decimal point.

They're also aware of how much is in the pot. If there's a million bucks in there already, it may pay to throw in another hundred thousand to protect the investment, even if you don't have that great a hand.

That's the kind of attitude the natural-born salespeople have. Pretty early on in the process, they have an idea of what the odds are that they'll get this sale. They can judge it by the reception they receive from the people they call on and what they hear back in terms of price, delivery schedule, and the other factors that influence a buying decision.

They know when it is appropriate to take a risk that makes them stand out from the crowd. In other words, paraphrasing the famous Kenny Rogers song, "you've got to know when to hold 'em, know when you could have sold 'em." Okay, so the poetry is bad, but the idea is good.

You have a prospect and the signals you're getting do not bode well for a sale. Why not go back to your manager and say, look, this is a big account. Let's do something a little risky.

I know a guy who was losing business to cheaper overseas manufacturers of a component. So he arranged with his boss to actually assemble the component with other parts of the product the client manufactured and ship it to them that way.

The client bought it. The salesman won the account back, and used that procedure to make sales with other companies.

It was a risky offer. His company had to change its production line to accommodate this new assembly. It had to hire people. And it had to assure the quality of the assembled product. But when the firm measured the risk against the potential rewards, it decided to go with its sales rep's instincts—and picked up a lot of business in the process.

Would you have done the same thing? Do you do any (many) of the things natural-born salespeople do? You won't become a natural-born salesperson just by following the tips in this book, but I truly believe your sales will increase and so will your level of satisfaction with your job and your life.

Besides, what's the risk?

WHAT TO TAKE FROM THIS CHAPTER

Entrepreneur Richard Branson, who created the Virgin brand of companies, says: "Success in business never comes from inaction. In business as in life, you can't be afraid to do the wrong thing. Success requires sales people to occasionally stick their necks out."

That doesn't mean be foolhardy. Know the risk/reward ratio to determine how far out your neck should go—if at all.

Even failure is good. At the very least, you'll learn a valuable lesson.

About the Author

Stephan Schiffman has trained more than 500,000 salespeople at firms such as AT&T Information Systems, JP Morgan, Chase, Motorola, and U.S. Healthcare. Mr. Schiffman, founder and chairman of DEI Management Group, is the author of *Cold Calling Techniques (That Really Work!)*, *The 25 Sales Habits of Highly Successful Salespeople*, and several other popular books on sales.

Do you have questions, comments, or suggestions regarding this book? Please share them with me! Write to me at this address: *sschiffman@steveschiffman.com*.

Index